Rea... Fox's excellent
...als

Here's ... ...inute Time Outs for Moms:

Robyn from British Columbia writes: "My life with four children is extremely busy and it's difficult to find time for personal devotions. My frustrations ended when my husband gave me a copy of *10-Minute Time Outs for Moms*. I have enjoyed it immensely. The Scriptures and stories are always what I need for that day. I feel this book is a gift not only for me, but for all busy moms. I'm recommending it to all my friends!"

Martha from California writes: "*10-Minute Time Outs for Moms* is an oasis for moms in the midst of a hectic day...If you need to take a few minutes to connect with the Lord and rejuvenate your spirit, this is a book that will help you do just that. Without a doubt this is one of the most delightful and inspiring devotionals for moms."

Wendy from Washington writes: "I found myself reading one selection to my 15 and 16-year-old daughters just because the ideas for that day were relevant to their lives. Adding this short reading into my daily time with God brightens and clarifies my relationship with Him."

Vikki from North Carolina writes: "Moms of toddlers to teens will find this book an oasis in a desert...An excellent gift for Mother's Day!! Buy one for yourself and one for a friend...you won't want to share!"

Peggy from Florida: "Grace's fervent love for Jesus and her genuine care for moms really shines in *10-Minute Time Outs For Moms*. Each real-life, inspiring devotion is a touching reminder of how God meets us as mothers right where we are. I highly recommend this book to moms everywhere. It's a perfect baby shower gift!

Kathleen from Saskatchewan writes: "*10-Minute Time Outs for Moms* works for grandmothers too! My daughter and family recently moved nearby and while it's an absolute delight, it's meant adjusting my own schedule. On baby-filled 'grandma days' I sometimes pick up Grace's book. Without fail, I am quickly ushered into the King's presence, refreshed and frequently reminded of the precious spiritual lessons only a child can teach."

~

Applause for
10-Minute Time Outs for Busy Women

How will you be remembered? As a woman who was always too busy...or as a woman who had a personal and passionate relationship with Jesus Christ? Let *10-Minute Time Outs for Busy Women* lead you to a lasting legacy of love.

Kendra Smiley
author of *High-Wire Mom* and *Aaron's Way*

10-Minute Time Outs for Busy Women addresses with extraordinary insight the ordinary pursuits and passions of today's busy women. From hamsters to heavenly hugs, from bathing suits to bothersome bugs, Grace shines God's penetrating flashlight along the path that turns up diamonds to enrich the heart.

Lt. Colonel Marlene Chase
Editor in Chief and Literary Secretary, Salvation Army

Warm, engaging, and right-on! Grace Fox speaks the language of the woman who does too much. Real-life stories supported by life-changing spiritual truths make *10-Minute Time Outs for Busy Women* an oasis that will refuel and recharge the spirit. A gifted writer, Grace draws busy women to reflect on their lives, challenging them to grow deeper in their relationship with God.

Margaret Gibb
President, Women Alive

Grace Fox has written an invaluable and inspirational book for busy and stressed women whether in the professional field or at home. The author gives an insightful and fresh look at our most important priority: nurturing and building our relationship with Jesus Christ. As one of these busy women, I highly recommend this book.

Diane Bish
host, *The Joy of Music* television series

If you're anything like me, you're busy, busy, *busy*. I feel as though most of life involves just trying to catch my breath before moving on to the next item on my to-do list! That's why I like *10-Minute Time Outs for Busy Women*. Grace Fox understands what busy women deal with every day, and she helps us stay on track in our spiritual lives. Grace reminds us profoundly in tiny bite-sized morsels that God's plan for us isn't about "just another thing to do" but about an awesomely rich and fulfilling relationship with him. Her words will help you remember and practice your faith all day long—no matter how full your schedule gets!

Ginger Kolbaba
Managing Editor, *Marriage Partnership* magazine

10-Minute Time Outs
for Busy Women

GRACE FOX

HARVEST HOUSE PUBLISHERS

EUGENE, OREGON

Cover by Koechel Peterson & Associates, Inc., Minneapolis, Minnesota

10-MINUTE TIME OUTS FOR BUSY WOMEN
Copyright © 2005 by Grace Fox
Published by Harvest House Publishers
Eugene, Oregon 97402
www.harvesthousepublishers.com

Library of Congress Cataloging-in-Publication Data
Fox, Grace, 1958-
    10-minute time outs for busy women / Grace Fox.
        p. cm.
    Includes bibliographical references.
    ISBN-13: 978-0-7369-1554-0
    ISBN-10: 0-7369-1554-0
    1. Christian women—Prayer-books and devotions—English. 2. Christian women—Religious life. I. Title: Ten minute time outs for busy women. II. Title.
    BV4844.F69 2005
    242'.643—dc22

                                                                        2004022172

Printed in the United States of America

                08   09   10   11   12   / DP-CF /   10   9   8   7   6   5

Ten days before I completed this manuscript, my cousin's wife, Tracey, passed away after battling cancer for nearly three years. She was 36 years old, the mother of two, a beautiful and fun-loving hair stylist.

Tracey's illness created within her an intense hunger to know God more intimately. Several months before her death, she took a month off work to rest her weary body, read the Bible, meditate, and pray. Her priorities changed. She wanted friends and family to know that work and life's busyness weren't important anymore. She discovered what mattered most: friendship with God and fellowship with others.

I dedicate this book to Tracey's legacy. May her passion for the Lord challenge and encourage us. And in the midst of our busy lives, may we, as Tracey did, make time for what matters most.

Acknowledgments

If not for my family, my friends, and the Harvest House staff, this book would have remained only in my imagination...

~ A big hug to Gene, who peeled me from my computer for mid-afternoon breaks and who shooed me into my office to type while he washed the dinner dishes night after night. Kudos to my kids—Matthew, Stephanie, and Kim—for praying and prodding me on.

~ A heartfelt thanks to friends who shared their stories with me and supported me through prayer. Words aren't adequate!

~ A gigantic thanks to Harvest House for all the behind-the-scenes labor. Your ministry has helped *10-Minute Time Outs for Busy Women* encourage readers to make time for what matters most.

~ And most important of all, thanks to the Lord for planting the idea for this book, and for giving the creativity and strength to bring it to reality. Friendship with Him is truly what matters most.

A Note from the Author

Dear Sisters,

Okay, I confess: I'm a busy woman. Perhaps that's because I'm a doer. I love being on the move and feeling as though I'm accomplishing something. Sitting still doesn't come naturally. Ask my husband, Gene.

One of our favorite winter evening activities is reading John Grisham novels together. I listen and do paint-by-number or make Christmas crafts while Gene reads aloud. We used to take turns, but we ran into a little problem.

Inevitably, five or six pages into my turn, my voice mutated into a drone, and I began skipping words. Before long, my head dropped to my chest. Mr. Grisham's lawyers stopped their cross-examinations. The witnesses fell silent. And my poor husband sat there, wondering whether he should tuck me in or wake me up.

Sailing is another favorite pastime, but it also presents a challenge. Granted, a gentle sail on a warm summer day is restful...for the body. After all, what can one do in a confined space except sit? But the mind—that's another story. Rather than relaxing, my brain goes bonkers, juggling all the things I could be doing or should be doing at home.

Occasionally, my "doer" mentality gets me into trouble. I volunteer for one too many commitments. I accept one too many invitations. I say yes once too often. What happens? My panic rises and my focus blurs.

But not all my busyness results from choice. I've experienced seasons when I've felt like a lunatic hamster on a treadmill that wouldn't stop. Like when my second child faced multiple hospitalizations and surgeries. Or when my dad suffered a crippling stroke at the same time that our family was still unpacking boxes after a move. Circumstances left me panting for more hours per day.

Perhaps you can relate. Life is busy—too busy. We wish we could slow down long enough to catch our breath, savor a sunset, or read a recommended novel without feeling guilty, but alas! No such luck.

As I wrote this book, I often thought about Martha. Remember her? Jesus and His disciples dropped by her home for a visit one day. I can picture her buzzing from one task to the next—preparing the evening meal while ensuring that her guests were comfortable. All the while, her sister, Mary, sat at Jesus' feet.

Mary's inactivity didn't impress Martha, who decided to do something about it. After all, why should she do all the work while her sister just sat there, doing nothing productive? "Lord, don't you care that my sister has left me to do the work by myself?" she asked. "Tell her to help me."

Jesus' response challenged her. "Martha, Martha," the Lord answered. "You are worried and upset about many things, but only one thing is needed. Mary has chosen what is better, and it will not be taken away from her" (Luke 10:40-42).

I wonder how Martha responded. Did she ignore Jesus' words and carry on, frustrated and stressed? Or did she listen? Did she hear His words and take them to heart?

We're often prone to let busyness dictate our daily schedules, but according to Jesus, that's not what He wants for our lives. Granted, He wants us to be faithful in our responsibilities, but He desires something more. He wants our hearts to be focused on Him. He wants us to sit at His feet, to hear His voice, to absorb what He says.

As I typed day after day, the Lord impressed one thought on my mind: "In the midst of the busyness, *make time for what matters most.*" What is that? It's cultivating our relationship with Him. Practicing His presence moment by moment. Discovering truths that strengthen our understanding of who He is and what's important to Him, and then applying those truths to our lives so others will see Him living in us.

In eternity's light, these things matter most. The choices we make depend on them. The legacy we leave hinges on them.

As you read this book, use the *Upward Gaze* to focus your thoughts on God's character. Ask Him to reveal His truth through the story. Apply that truth to your own life by answering the *Inward Glimpse* questions. Use the *Outward Glance* prayer to pray for yourself or another busy woman in your life—your mom, sister, best friend, or employer. Or use it as a guide in praying for your spouse or children, or anyone else for that matter! Finally, take *One More Peek* into God's Word and allow it to encourage or change you.

I pray that the Holy Spirit will breathe life into the words on these pages as you read them. May you share Mary's delight as you take a time-out at Jesus' feet. May you hear His heart as He reveals what matters most.

I know you're busy—if not, you wouldn't be holding this book. But if you find time, I'd love to hear from you. Tell me what God's doing in your life! You can reach me through my website: www.gracefox.com.

Know you are loved,
Grace

Hamster Lessons

"For I know the plans I have for you," declares the LORD, "plans to prosper you and not to harm you, plans to give you hope and a future."

JEREMIAH 29:11

Upward Gaze

Father, I praise You for having a purpose for my life. In Your wisdom and sovereignty You planned my days, long before my birth. Your thoughts toward me are precious (Psalm 139:16-17). I trust You to show me Your purpose and enable me to pursue it. Amen.

~

Rattle, rattle, rattle, rattle. The noise interrupted my sleep for the third consecutive night. I opened my eyes and caught the alarm clock's red digits staring at me through the darkness. It was 2:30 A.M.—an hour when a house and its occupants should be silent or snoring. *Should* be. But down the hall, down two flights of stairs, and across the family room, a furry resident—our pet hamster—had decided to wake up and work out. Again.

Worried that the hamster would grow bored sitting in its cage, our kids had purchased and installed a plastic treadmill several days earlier. The creature loved it. Each night, long after our family had fallen asleep, it climbed aboard the yellow wheel and set it spinning round and round and round. Each morning, we found the critter fast asleep in the corner of its cage, exhausted after its nocturnal fitness session.

Have you ever felt like the hamster? I have. And believe me, my exhaustion isn't a result of working out at the gym. One could only wish! Nope, my life sometimes resembles the hamster on its treadmill: Work, work, work, collapse. Work, work, work, collapse.

I'm not the only female who occasionally feels this way. While traveling on a plane recently, I sat beside a woman in her mid-thirties. She'd buried her nose in a book whose cover showed a cartoon woman in high heels frantically trying to juggle several grocery bags while a crying toddler pulled at her skirt. I chuckled at the scene and asked, "Is that a good book?"

The woman looked up and nodded. "My sister bought it for me. She thinks I need it." She rolled her eyes and grinned. "I can't imagine why. After all, I only have three kids under 12. I volunteer in their schools. I serve on five committees. I work full-time outside my home. I'm planning to start nurse's training in a few months. And—" She drew a deep breath before her grand finale. "I own a 100-pound dysfunctional Rottweiler."

"Is that all?" I said. She looked at me in disbelief, but when she realized that I was joking, she grinned again.

"Yep. That's all I can handle. Well, sometimes I feel like it's more than I can handle. I'm busier than I want to be, but I don't know how to stop."

Too often our lives resemble that of my family's furry friend. We race from meeting to meeting. We run from one obligation to the next. We wish the day held more hours so we could accomplish everything on our to-do list. Sometimes our activities are necessary, like caring for our children or our elderly parents, or working to put food on the table. Sometimes, however, our activities make us appear busy when we're actually racing nowhere and accomplishing nothing. So what's a woman to do?

In his book *The Purpose-Driven Life*, author Rick Warren suggests that we ask ourselves, *Does this activity help me fulfill one of God's purposes for my life?* If the answer is yes, we should embrace it with gusto. If the answer is no, we should release it—without guilt. Sounds simple, doesn't it? In truth, determining God's purposes may take some serious soul-searching and a conscientious commitment to pursue them no matter what. We may have to thin our existing obligations or learn to say no, but the effort brings rewards.

According to Warren, streamlining our activities to pursue God's purposes simplifies and focuses our lives. "It concentrates our effort and energy on what's important," he writes. "You become effective by being selective." When we eliminate everything except that which matters most, we become productive rather than simply busy. The difference is huge.

God never intended our lives to mimic the hamster on the treadmill. He wants us to enjoy abundant, fruitful life. Let's begin today!

Inward Glimpse

Dear Father, thank You for having a purpose for my life. Help me know and pursue it so I might spend my days engaged in meaningful activity rather than fruitless busyness. Amen.

- What do you believe God's purposes are for your life?
- What changes must you make to pursue those purposes?

Outward Glance

Heavenly Father, thank You for teaching _____ Your ways. Please help her live wisely, making the most of every opportunity (Ephesians 5:15-16). Help her press on to embrace the purpose for which Christ Jesus took hold of her (Philippians 3:12). I ask these things in Jesus' name. Amen.

One More Peek

You will keep in perfect peace
  him whose mind is steadfast,
  because he trusts in you (Isaiah 26:3).

Bathing Suits
and Snowflakes

Yet, O LORD, you are our Father.
We are the clay, you are the potter;
we are all the work of your hand.

ISAIAH 64:8

Upward Gaze

Dear Father, You created my inmost being; You knit me together in my mother's womb. I praise You because I am fearfully and wonderfully made. Your works are wonderful, I know that very well (Psalm 139:13-14). Amen.

~

A friend in her mid-fifties burst into giggles while browsing for a birthday card. "Listen to this one," she said. "At our age, there are only two things we should avoid: pizza and bathing suits."

I beg to differ on one point: Pizza still sounds good to me. Steamy, spicy, cheesy pizza—yum!

But I agree with the bathing suit issue. I've yet to find a suit that makes me look as good as pizza tastes—steamy and spicy. At my age, the only suits I find make me look cheesy.

It's bathing suit season as I write this. I scanned the selection in a mail-order catalog and noticed little symbols beside each picture. Inverted triangles represent bust-enhancing suits. The I-shapes give the illusion of a waistline. The A-shapes make hips appear smaller. The X-shapes make women look balanced (whatever that means). And the asterisks represent suits for women with special body needs. Something for everyone, and good thing because every body is uniquely shaped.

Our uniqueness extends way beyond physical appearance—body shape, eye color, hair color, height, weight, and so forth. Every woman on the face of this earth possesses a one-of-a-kind blend of personality traits, interests, and talents. That mix contributes to the role we play in our community. Some women teach school or music lessons. Others provide foster care for needy children. Some serve in the military or as police officers. Others enjoy farming. The list goes on forever.

Our individuality reminds me of snowflakes. Wilson Bentley, the first person to photograph a single snow crystal, discovered snowflakes' unique design through extensive research. In his lifetime, he captured more than 5000 of them and found no two alike. He explains his motivation:

> Under a microscope, I found that snowflakes were miracles of beauty; and it seemed a shame that this beauty should not be seen and appreciated by others. Every crystal was a masterpiece of design and no one design was ever repeated. When a snowflake melted, that design was forever lost. Just that much beauty was gone, without leaving any record behind.

Bentley saw snowflakes as miracles of beauty, masterpieces of design. The same sentiment applies to us! We are miracles of beauty, masterpieces of God's design. And, as with snowflakes, something is lost when no one sees or appreciates this beauty.

Sometimes we hide our beauty without realizing it. We compare ourselves to other women and feel inferior. We think others won't like us as we are, so we wear a façade. We hesitate to try new activities because we're afraid of failing. We don't initiate or respond to new relationships because we fear rejection. We allow feelings of inadequacy to rule, and we decline opportunities to use our interests and abilities to serve others. By doing so, we hide our beauty—the Creator's masterpiece of design. And when we're gone, our unique design is forever lost without leaving a trace.

God has given us our specific personalities, interests, and talents for a reason—He wants to accomplish life-changing, earth-shattering, society-rattling tasks through us. He wants to heal the hurting, comfort the mourning, and love the unlovely. He wants to impact the world for Jesus Christ. If we hide our beauty, we hinder His work. But when we accept ourselves the way He's put us together and participate in what He wants to do, we make Him smile. And not only that, but our lives touch family, neighbors, coworkers, our church and community, and just maybe the whole world.

Our body shapes differ. Our personalities differ. Our interests and giftedness differ. And that's okay. Our heavenly Father, the one who creates miracles of beauty, makes no mistakes. He surveys His work and says, "It is good." And that means you, my one-of-a-kind friend.

Inward Glimpse

Dear Father, thank You for making me a miracle of beauty. Give me a thankful heart for Your design. Amen.

- What are your talents? How can you use them to bless others and build God's kingdom?
- Look for opportunities to encourage at least three women this week. Write a little note, say a kind word, make a surprise phone call. Let them know they're appreciated.

Outward Glance

Lord, I pray that _____ will embrace the way You knit her in her mother's womb. Help her understand and appreciate her uniqueness. And as she does, please bless her, be gracious to her, and cause Your face to shine on her that Your ways may be known on the earth and Your salvation to all nations (Psalm 67:1-2). Amen.

One More Peek

How great is the love the Father has lavished on us, that we should be called the children of God! And that is what we are! (1 John 3:1).

Follow the Chart

All Scripture is God-breathed and is useful for teaching, rebuking, correcting and training in righteousness, so that the man of God may be thoroughly equipped for every good work.

2 TIMOTHY 3:16-17

Upward Gaze

Father, all men are like grass, and all their glory is like the flowers of the field; the grass withers and the flowers fall, but Your Word stands forever (1 Peter 1:24-25). Thank You for giving us Your unchanging Word to show us how to navigate life. Amen.

~

Sailing is a favorite activity at the camp where we live and work. But to sail safely in our harbor and the outlying regions, we follow a strict rule—the skippers must be fully acquainted with the local tides and currents. They must also know where the underwater rocks are located.

Knowing the location of the rocks is critical. If a boat rams one, it could easily break a rudder or rip a hull. To ensure safety, each skipper uses a chart that shows where these boulders are hidden.

Let's pretend that an overly confident skipper joins our ranks. She calls herself a mariner, alright, but her skill leaves something to be desired, especially in unfamiliar territory. She struts to the dock, unties the ropes, and climbs into the boat. We offer her a nautical chart. "A map? Who needs a map?" she says. "I'll be fine. Watch me."

And so we stand on the dock and watch. In fact, we watch the ill-fated sailboat cruise headlong into one of those hidden rocks. *Ker-runch!*

"Oops!" she calls. She thrusts the engine into reverse. "Don't worry—just minor damage!" Away she goes again. *Slam!* She smacks into another one. "No problem! I can do this!" Like a ricocheting rubber ball, she bounces from one rock to the next, incurring more and more damage.

The scene dumbfounds us. *Doesn't this self-confident skipper see certain shipwreck ahead? Doesn't she understand that the chart was designed by experts who know the territory and are concerned for her safety? How can anyone be so foolish?*

The scene I've described sounds ludicrous. It would never happen. Or would it?

Actually, it happens every day. Not at our camp, of course. And not with sailboats. In reality, it replays itself in women's lives.

"The Bible? Who needs the Bible?" a woman says. "I can handle life on my own." Off she sails into life's harbor. Trouble is, the harbor is riddled with rocks such as worry, anger, finances, marriage, sex, and sin. And without God's Word, the chart for life, she can't know the secret to safe navigation.

Before long, the woman careens into worry. The chart says, "Do not be anxious about anything, but in everything, by prayer and petition, with thanksgiving, present your requests to God" (Philippians 4:6). But she ignores the chart and instead battles sleepless nights and ulcers and fear.

She hasn't recovered from worry before she collides with anger. The chart says, "Do not let the sun go down while you are still angry" (Ephesians 4:26). Ignoring the instruction, she buries bitterness deep within her heart and incurs more damage. And so she goes, zigzagging through the harbor, believing she can navigate without God's directives and wondering why her journey seems disaster stricken.

Like that woman, we too have a choice. We can choose to navigate life in our own wisdom or follow the chart—God's Word. We can rest assured that it never changes and that it's written with our best interest in mind. Surely the last option—following the chart—is best. After all, God designed it Himself. And He's the expert on life's principles and practices.

Inward Glimpse

Dear Father, thank You for giving me Your chart for life. Help me follow it rather than my own whims and wishes. Amen.

- How has God's Word helped you navigate life's rock-riddled waters?
- If you've hit a rock and incurred damage, don't worry. God can repair the damage and set you on your way again. Write a prayer asking Him to help you follow His Word from now on.

Outward Glance

Father, I pray that _____ will present herself to you as a worker who does not need to be ashamed and one who correctly handles Your Word (2 Timothy 2:15). Sustain her according to Your Word that she may live. Uphold her that she might be safe, that she might always have regard for Your decrees (Psalm 119:116-117). Amen.

One More Peek

Your word is a lamp to my feet
   and a light for my path (Psalm 119:105).

Security

Blessed is he whose help is the God of Jacob,
whose hope is in the LORD his God.

PSALM 146:5

Upward Gaze

God, I praise You for being my refuge and strength, an ever present help in trouble. I will not fear even though the earth gives way and the mountains slip into the sea (Psalm 46:1-2). Amen.

⁓

Security is a word we often hear, especially since 9/11. People want to know their lives are guarded. They want to feel safe.

I can relate. I'm concerned for my loved ones' security too. When my children were little, I controlled where they went and who they played with. As a responsible mother, I claimed a measure of responsibility for their well-being. But now they're young adults. Two have already left home. I have no idea what they're doing or when and where they're doing it. I have no way to ensure their safety.

Our 21-year-old son, Matt, volunteers aboard a ministry ship that travels from port to port around the world. A recent phone conversation with him reminded me of this truth.

"There's something you should know," Matt said.

"What is it?" I asked, my curiosity rising.

"Well…about two weeks ago, a friend and I were almost robbed at gunpoint."

I wasn't sure I'd heard him correctly. "Did you say *gunpoint?*" My mind raced, trying to comprehend his words.

"Yeah." Matt explained that he and his friend had been sitting on a park bench in Fort-de-France, Martinique, when a drunk stranger approached them, engaged them in small talk, and asked for money. Matt realized the man was also high on drugs. Matt did not want to fuel the man's addiction, so he denied the request. The stranger dropped his voice and said, "I have a gun."

Before Matt could decide whether or not to call the man's bluff, another fellow sauntered by. Matt called to him, but as he approached the threesome, the first stranger pulled the gun from his pocket. The newcomer could have fled at that moment. Instead, he planted himself between the robber and the two foreigners. His quick thinking and selfless action allowed Matt and his friend to run to safety.

Matt's experience makes me shudder. At the same time, I thank God for His protection. Who else could have sent a rescuer willing to interrupt an armed robbery and plant himself inches from a gun barrel?

As I write this, my 19-year-old daughter is working in a town about a thousand miles from home. My 17-year-old daughter is traveling home from Mexico after teaching Bible clubs for two weeks. My kids thrive on new experiences, and they've been blessed with opportunities to serve the Lord in unique ways and places.

Regardless of the world's political situation, I am obliged and privileged to let them go where God calls them. Is that easy? No. Not a day goes by without my wondering how they're coping with relationships, works, and practical things like managing their money, keeping house, and cooking. And not a morning passes when I don't ask God to be their security.

God alone can guard my loved ones and provide the security they need in this insecure world. That doesn't mean nothing bad will ever happen to them, but it *does* mean He'll be with them in times of trouble. He'll do the same for you and yours.

When we relinquish control and acknowledge that God is our loved ones' keeper and the only one who can provide true security, we experience peace and know the privilege of watching God use them to accomplish His purposes.

Inward Glimpse

Dear Father, thank You for being my security. Help me walk in that knowledge and encourage others to do the same. Amen.

- Name a situation that's difficult to surrender to God's keeping. What do you think might happen if you relinquish control?
- Read the hymn "Anywhere with Jesus." What's the secret to fearlessness?

Outward Glance

Father, I pray that _____ will make You her dwelling and refuge. Let no harm befall her and no disaster come near her tent. Command Your angels to guard her in all her ways (Psalm 91:9-11). Teach her to rest in Your shadow and trust fully in You (Psalm 91:1-2). Amen.

One More Peek

"Because he loves me," says the LORD, *"I will rescue him;*
*   I will protect him, for he acknowledges my name.*
He will call upon me, and I will answer him;
*   I will be with him in trouble,*
*   I will deliver him and honor him.*
With long life will I satisfy him
*   and show him my salvation"* (Psalm 91:14-15).

Anywhere with Jesus

Jessie B. Pounds

Anywhere with Jesus I can safely go;
Anywhere He leads me in this world below;
Anywhere without Him dearest joys would fade;
Anywhere with Jesus I am not afraid.

Anywhere with Jesus I am not alone;
Other friends may fail me, He is still my own;
Though His hand may lead me over dreary ways,
Anywhere with Jesus is a house of praise.

Anywhere with Jesus I can go to sleep,
When the darkening shadows round about me creep;
Knowing I shall waken never more to roam,
Anywhere with Jesus will be home, sweet home.

Anywhere! Anywhere! Fear I cannot know;
Anywhere with Jesus I can safely go.

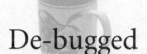

De-bugged

He makes me lie down in green pastures,
he leads me beside quiet waters.

PSALM 23:2

Upward Gaze

Father, my soul finds rest in You alone. You are my hope, my salvation, my rock, and my fortress (Psalm 62:2,5). You have shown me the path of life. Your presence fills me with joy. Your right hand fills me with eternal pleasures (Psalm 16:11). Amen.

∼

Minor irritations dot our lives. When we encounter them, we often say we're "bugged." And one night, not too long ago, a friend was bugged big-time...

Kristi tugged on her bedcovers and glanced at the alarm clock—1:28 A.M. She'd retired nearly three hours earlier but hadn't slept yet. Over and over, her mind rehashed the previous night's conversation with her husband.

"I have some good news and some bad news," he said at dinner. "The good news is…I've been offered a promotion. Great pay. Nice perks." He paused, studying Kristi's face. "The bad news is…it means moving to Los Angeles."

Kristi stared. "Los Angeles? You must be kidding!" A weak laugh escaped her lips.

"Not kidding," he said. "I think we can handle it. What do you think?"

What did she think? They'd built their dream home only three years earlier. Located on ten wooded acres, the yard provided a natural playground for their kids. Both sets of grandparents lived nearby. The children enjoyed their school. She loved having coffee with her friends.

"What do I think? I think you've already made your decision," Kristi said. She rose from the table and began clearing dirty dishes. Her husband rose too and left the room.

Kristi adjusted her pillow again. Relocating would be difficult, but she wasn't opposed to it. It was her husband's approach that bugged her.

Why did he dump the news on me like that? He gave me no forewarning. He's pulled similar stunts, but this one tops them all. Her irritation grew. A long, sleepless night lay ahead.

Sound familiar? Our circumstances might be different from Kristi's, but they still bug us. Sometimes they're petty: The hairdresser cuts our hair too short or the babysitter arrives ten minutes late. Sometimes they're bigger: We anticipate a romantic evening with hubby, but his boss asks him to work overtime. Perhaps our personality clashes with a coworker's, and simply being in the same room creates tension. What happens? Our negative emotions steal our rest—physical, emotional, and spiritual.

In his book *A Shepherd Looks at Psalm 23*, Phillip Keller says that sheep react to irritants in a similar way. Being "bugged" by flies or parasites makes rest nearly impossible for them. Their helpless state causes them to be "up and on their feet, stamping their legs, shaking their heads, ready to rush off into the bush for relief from the pests."

When annoyances bug us, we don't normally stamp our legs, shake our heads, and rush off into the bush. (We might feel like it sometimes, though!) Instead, we retreat behind stony silence, speak words we later regret, or toss and turn at night. Studying God's Word and praying become nearly impossible because our thoughts flit from one to another as we stew about our situation.

Just as a diligent shepherd recognizes his sheep's discomfort and rushes to their rescue, so God, our Shepherd, sees our plight. He wants to remedy it so we can once again enjoy contentment and peace. How does He do that? Through His Holy Spirit, who lives within us. Keller explains the process:

> When I turn to Him and expose the problem to Him, allowing Him to see that I have a dilemma, a difficulty, a disagreeable experience beyond my control, He comes to assist. Often a helpful approach is simply to say aloud, "O Master, this is beyond me—I can't cope with it—it's bugging me—I can't rest—please take over!"
>
> Then He does take over in His own wondrous way. He applies the healing, soothing, effective antidote of His own person and presence to my particular problem. There immediately comes into my consciousness the awareness of His dealing with the difficulty in a way I had not anticipated. And because of the assurance that He has become active on my behalf, there steals over me a sense of quiet contentment. I am then able to lie down in peace and rest. All because of what He does.[1]

Next time we're feeling bugged and restless, we can remember Keller's insight. We can admit our helplessness to resolve the problem and know that our Shepherd will apply the soothing reality of His presence in us so we can lie down and rest.

Inward Glimpse

Dear Father, thank You for knowing how to free me from irritations. Help me to rest in the knowledge of Your presence in me. Amen.

- What frustrations are preventing you from enjoying rest? Write a prayer asking the Good Shepherd to take over and apply the necessary healing.
- Memorize today's key verse.

Outward Glance

Dear Father, teach _____ to wait in hope for You. Help her understand that You are her help and shield. May her heart rejoice for trusting in Your holy name. And may Your unfailing love rest upon her (Psalm 33:20-22). Amen.

One More Peek

I will lie down and sleep in peace,
  for you alone, O LORD,
  make me dwell in safety (Psalm 4:8).

Extinguish the Fire

Likewise the tongue is a small part of the body, but it makes great boasts. Consider what a great forest is set on fire by a small spark.

JAMES 3:5

Upward Gaze

God, I praise You because Your words are so much better than mine! They are totally trustworthy (2 Samuel 7:28). They are flawless, like silver refined in a furnace of clay, purified seven times (Psalm 12:6). Thanks for showing me Your standard for my speech. Amen.

～

The disaster began in August of 2003 when a single stray spark landed on dry grass in southern British Columbia. A breeze fanned it into a flame. Within days, heat and high winds blew it into an inferno. The Okanagan fire blazed through the forest at nearly 300 feet per minute and chased 30,000 residents from their homes. Tree after tree exploded in its path. Hour by hour the flames spread, dumped more ash, devoured more homes, and terrorized more victims. If only that spark had been contained!

James mentions sparks and forest fires when he teaches about the tongue's power. "Likewise the tongue is a small part of the body, but it makes great boasts. Consider what a great forest is set on fire by a small spark. The tongue also is a fire, a world of evil among the parts of the body. It corrupts the whole person, sets the whole course of his life on fire, and is itself set on fire by hell" (James 3:5-6).

Wow! Is that strong language or what? James uses it for good reason. Like an out-of-control fire, our tongue's destructive potential is *huge!* Ask Janet. She experienced the flames firsthand.

Janet's in her mid-thirties now, but she still remembers her parents' words: "Leave me alone—I don't have time for you now." "I'll love you if you're a good girl." "You're so difficult! Sometimes I wish you'd never been born."

Those words colored Janet's understanding of her value and purpose. They left her feeling insecure, unlovable, and in turn, unable to accept and love others. True to James' words, the tongue ignited a fire that affected the course of her life.

Scripture tells us to extinguish the flame. How is this done? By refusing to speak critical or harsh comments, by eliminating sarcasm and inappropriate humor from our conversation, and by not participating in gossip.

A magazine article told of two women who visited a restaurant for lunch. They popped into the restroom to reapply their lipstick, and one gal launched into a two-minute tirade about a mutual coworker. When she finished speaking, a stall door opened, and out walked that coworker. The three stared at each other in awkward silence. The tearful coworker then fled the scene and later resigned her position.[2]

The tongue—a fire with destructive potential. But hey, not all fires are bad.

We once owned a lakefront home with a big, flat yard—the perfect site for hosting parties. On summer evenings, we invited folks to swim and then sit around the fire pit. We roasted marshmallows, told jokes and stories, sang silly camp songs, and enjoyed each other's company. Many fond memories were created around that snapping, crackling fire.

Now we work at a Christian camp. Without exception, kids and adults alike relish the evening campfires. They represent fun and fellowship. They provide an escape, a time of reflection, relaxation, and refreshment for busy or burdened souls.

Yes, our tongues are a fire, but they don't have to destroy. We can use them to speak kind words to our children. We can use them to express appreciation to those who labor behind the scenes—the church or school janitor, a caregiver, a gardener. We can use them to praise the Lord even when we don't feel like it, and to pray for others.

Sounds easy, doesn't it? Well, it's not! If left to our own devices, we'd all become professional flame throwers. God knows that, so He sent His Holy Spirit to teach us how to extinguish the fire. When we're tempted to let sparks fly through criticism, complaining, and gossip, we can call on Him for help. By His power, our tongues can ignite hope and joy in those around us. And we'll never be left wishing, *If only that spark had been contained!*

Inward Glimpse

Dear Father, thank You for revealing my tongue's potential. Guard my tongue from causing damage and use it for Your glory. Amen.

- What words or expressions come from your mouth when you're tired or feeling angry? What changes would you like to make?
- Write a prayer asking the Holy Spirit to make you keenly aware of your words. Ask Him to make your words healing and helpful to others.

Outward Glance

Father, I pray that no unwholesome talk would come from _____'s mouth. Teach her to speak only what's helpful for building others up according to their needs (Ephesians 4:29). May her conversation be grace-filled, seasoned with salt, and may she always know how to answer everyone (Colossians 4:6). Amen.

One More Peek

A man finds joy in giving an apt reply—
   and how good is a timely word! (Proverbs 15:23).

Promise Keeper

Your word, O LORD, is eternal;
it stands firm in the heavens.
Your faithfulness continues through all generations;
you established the earth, and it endures.

PSALM 119:89-90

Upward Gaze

Almighty God, there is no God like You in heaven or on earth—You keep Your covenant of love with Your servants who continue wholeheartedly in Your way. Just as You kept Your promise to David, so You will keep Your promises to me today. With Your mouth You promise and with Your hand You fulfill it (2 Chronicles 6:14-15). Amen.

❧

"Do ya wanna know my secret?" whispers an eight-year-old to her best friend.

"Yes! Tell me!" the friend says.

"Promise you won't tell anyone?"

"I promise."

"Cross your heart?"

"Cross my heart."

Vows complete, the secret is shared. Later that day, the scene repeats itself. "Hey! Ya wanna know a secret?" whispers the friend to another girl.

Oh, how well I remember scenes like that—promises lightly made and quickly broken. But kids aren't the only ones who break promises. Grown-ups do it too.

A disillusioned husband breaks his "till death do us part" marriage vows. He walks away, leaving his wife and children with broken hearts and unanswered questions. An overworked mother promises to sew her daughter's prom dress. But at day's end, she's too exhausted to think straight, let alone sew a straight seam. A father promises to attend his son's ball game, but work obligations receive priority. The boy waits and watches for his dad, and then he stifles his disappointment...again.

In all likelihood, we've experienced the disappointment that accompanies broken promises. Or perhaps we've disappointed others. Isn't it reassuring to know that God doesn't behave as people do? Scripture contains many reminders about God's faithfulness to fulfill His covenants to His children. And because He's sinless, He can't lie. Therefore, He always, *always* keeps His word. He will never disappoint us by failing to keep His promises.

So what does that mean in the nitty-gritty of everyday life? For starters, when God guarantees His presence wherever we go, He means it. Therefore, if we're walking in obedience to His commands, we can face a job transfer with confidence. We can hit middle age and return to college knowing we're not alone. We can board a plane and fly overseas assured of His companionship.

When God pledges to grant wisdom to those who ask for it, He keeps His word. We can call on Him when our kids' behavior baffles us. We can holler for help when an elderly parent refuses much-needed assistance. We can ask for direction when our journey brings us to a fork in the road and we don't know which way to travel.

God always fulfills His promises. Sometimes, however, He seems to have broken His word to us. Financial struggles leave us wondering why

He isn't providing for our needs. Chronic illness makes us wonder why He isn't healing us. We feel betrayed. Our trust wavers. Our faith falters. In such instances, we must remember that God works on an eternal timetable, not one limited by our finite days.

I wonder if the Old Testament character Abraham felt as though God had broken His promise. After all, God had pledged to give him as many descendants as the grains of sand on the seashore, but in his old age, Abraham's wife still hadn't borne a child. As the wrinkled, grey-haired man weighed the promise against the harsh reality of his wife's barren womb, perhaps he wondered if God had lied.

As modern-day observers, however, we follow Abraham's account and know that God kept His word. He was simply working according to His divine schedule—the Jewish nation's existence proves it.

The knowledge that God always fulfills His promises enables us to face each challenge with courage, confidence, and joy. Whatever your need is today, I pray that He will bring to your mind a promise to match it, the peace to wait for His timing, and the privilege of watching Him fulfill it.

Inward Glimpse

Heavenly Father, thank You for keeping Your promises. Help me reflect Your character to others by keeping my promises too. Amen.

- Have you made a promise but not fulfilled it? Make a commitment to do it soon.
- Find a Bible promise that applies to whatever need you're facing right now. Write it on a recipe card and post it where you can see it several times a day.

Outward Glance

Heavenly Father, Your words are flawless, like silver refined in a furnace of clay, purified seven times. I pray that _____'s words will be pure and flawless like Yours

(Psalm 12:6). Guard her from making promises that she cannot fulfill. May her words always be above reproach, spoken from a heart of integrity. Amen.

One More Peek

Your promises have been thoroughly tested,
  and your servant loves them (Psalm 119:140).

Abby

This is love: not that we loved God, but that he loved us and sent his Son as an atoning sacrifice for our sins. Dear friends, since God so loved us, we also ought to love one another.

1 JOHN 4:10-11

Upward Gaze

Heavenly Father, I praise You for being love itself (1 John 4:16). You showed Your love by sending Your only begotten Son into the world so that the world might have life (1 John 4:9). Thank You for Your example. Amen.

~

Peggy sat at her kitchen table, sipping coffee and pondering the words she'd read in her Bible. *Since God so loved us, we also ought to love one another.* The thought of His love for her filled her heart with gratitude. At the same time, however, she sensed a duty to respond by sharing it with others. "Help me love someone today," she prayed. Moments later she began tackling her day's writing goals.

The phone rang later that morning. "Abby's home from the hospital," said a neighbor. "She's crying and wants to speak with your husband."

Ah, Abby—the woman who lived across the street from Peggy. The alcoholic who shared her house with several men at a time. The one whose lifestyle forced her eight-year-old daughter to seek shelter at Grandma's house for weeks, sometimes months.

When one boyfriend moved out several days prior, Abby had gone to his workplace in a drunken rage and begged him to return. A fight ensued. Police arrived and tried to restrain Abby, but she fought them too. The scuffle resulted in her suffering a broken arm. After spending several days in jail and the hospital, Abby was home and wanting to speak with Peggy's husband, a pastor.

Peggy phoned her husband but discovered that other obligations prevented him from coming. Feeling as though she'd done what she could to help Abby, Peggy returned to her computer keyboard. That's when she sensed the Lord speaking.

His question was simple and direct: *What did you pray this morning?*

Peggy stopped typing and recalled her prayer: *Help me love someone today*. She responded with instant obedience. "You're right, Lord! I'll go." Moments later, she entered Abby's house. She embraced the crying woman, who in turn, placed her head on Peggy's chest.

"I'm filthy," Abby said through her sobs. "I haven't bathed for days…"

"I'll bathe you," Peggy volunteered. She ran warm water into the bathtub and then helped Abby climb in, scrubbed her back, and washed her matted hair. As she did so, she began telling the woman about Jesus' love for her.

"The dirt on your body is like sin," said Peggy. "Water can wash the dirt away but only Jesus can wash away your sin. He wants to do that for you. He wants to make you clean on the inside and turn your whole life around." The woman listened but said nothing.

Peggy returned home after she'd settled Abby. Were her efforts worthwhile? She would never know. But she *did* know that, regardless of Abby's response, she had done what God required. She'd shared His love with her neighbor that day, and she felt an undeniable joy.

Our finite minds have difficulty wrapping themselves around God's love. We hear about it. We sing about it. We thank Him for it. But really understanding its measure is difficult. And expressing it is even more challenging for us, especially when those needing it most are considered unlovely or "high maintenance" by society's standards. Showing practical deeds of kindness is much easier when the recipient shows gratitude or loves us in return. But that's not what God did. According to Scripture, He loved us even while we were still sinners—when there wasn't a hope of our returning His love or at least saying thanks.

Mother Teresa challenged us to follow Jesus' example:

> The chance to share our love with others is a gift from God. May it be for us just as it was for Jesus. Let's love one another as He has loved us. Let's love one another with undivided love. Let's experience the joy of loving God and loving one another.

Sometimes, we regard meeting another's need as a duty or interference, an obligation or inconvenience. But if we remember God's command to love others as He loves us, we too can see the opportunity as a gift from Him—a chance to let His love flow through us and experience the joy that comes from obedience.

Inward Glimpse

Heavenly Father, thank You for loving me. Open my eyes to see opportunities to love others in the same way. Amen.

- List three practical ways you can share God's love with your family or friends within the next week.
- Ask God to give you the opportunity to love someone today. Record His answer.

Outward Glance

Dear Father, You've shown us the measure of Your love through Jesus Christ. Please help _____reflect Your love to others by showing compassion to those in need. Teach her to love not only with words and tongue, but with actions and in truth (1 John 3:16-18). Amen.

One More Peek

To love him with all your heart, with all your understanding and with all your strength, and to love your neighbor as yourself is more important than all burnt offerings and sacrifices (Mark 12:33).

Heavenly Hugs

*"But let him who boasts boast about this:
that he understands and knows me,
that I am the LORD, who exercises kindness,
justice and righteousness on earth,
for in these I delight," declares the LORD.*

JEREMIAH 9:24

Upward Gaze

Father, I praise You for demonstrating true kindness and love through the person of Jesus Christ. I've done nothing to deserve Your kindness, yet You freely gave it and even gave me eternal life. Thank You! (Titus 3:4-5). Amen.

∿

What's warmer than a hug when we're feeling sad or lonely? Not much. An affectionate squeeze encircles our body and embraces our heart. It makes us feel cared for, wanted, and valued.

We all need a hug once in a while. As for 20-year-old Maggie, well, hers was past due. One afternoon while driving along Montreal's busy highway network, she launched into a screaming match with her car's other occupant—God.

"I'm so lonely—I can't do this anymore!" she yelled.

I know how you feel, God seemed to reply. *But you've got Me.*

"That doesn't work," Maggie shouted. "You don't have arms!"

Six months earlier, Maggie had been accepted by a mission agency to work in Quebec. The organization assigned her to work with French-speaking people. Her role involved attending a French-speaking church and visiting new contacts that her pastor made. There was just one problem: Maggie couldn't speak their language.

Months passed. Maggie grew frustrated at her inability to hold meaningful discussions with others. *Really, I am smart, but I just can't get my thoughts out!* she wanted to say. She could talk about recipes and the weather and the time of day, but she couldn't be herself—a thinker, an analyzer, a woman invigorated by debate. She worried that people viewed her as a friendly airhead—a woman who smiled a lot but with little intellectual depth.

Cars whizzed past Maggie as she continued down the highway. *I've come here to serve You, God, and what happens? I end up feeling lost, like a ship adrift with no anchor.* She pulled into the church's driveway and parked her car. She forced a smile as she mentally prepared herself to sit through yet another meeting in a foreign language.

As Maggie entered the building, a young woman approached her. She recognized her as a mother of two small children—someone who, despite the language barrier, had displayed friendliness in the past through smiles and small talk. Now, without speaking a word, the woman threw her arms around Maggie and hugged her. And hugged her. And hugged her.

Maggie stood speechless. *Wow, God, I was wrong! You really do have arms!*

God *does* have arms—yours and mine, or in Maggie's case, the young French mother's. He wants to hug the hurting, and He does that through His children.

Sometimes that means extending literal, physical hugs. A single mom once told me that she often craves a hearty squeeze. I tucked that into my memory bank and make a point of embracing her each time we meet. Seniors love hugs too. And our spouse and kids can't get enough.

But we can embrace others in God's love in other ways too. We can extend emotional hugs by reading our child's favorite bedtime story again…and again…and again. By taking a new immigrant grocery shopping or helping her register her children at school. By paying for a less fortunate boy or girl to attend summer camp or by providing meals to a family whose mother has just given birth. By sending a care package to a college student far from home or writing a soldier serving overseas.

Sometimes we long for heavenly hugs but don't receive them as quickly as we wish we would. We wonder if God has arms, and if He does, why He doesn't use them. In those situations, God might be allowing us to experience pain so that we can understand another person's grief. When that happens, we can ask God to help us see beyond our own needs and to recognize, as the French woman did, the one who needs a hug from heaven.

Opportunities surround us. May God embrace someone through our arms today!

Inward Glimpse

Dear Father, thank You for sending hugs through Your people. Help me recognize those who need reassurance of Your love. Amen.

- Ask the Lord to send someone across your path today who needs a hug.
- List three ways in which you can be God's arms in your community, and then put those ideas into action.

Outward Glance

Father, I pray that _____ will allow Your Holy Spirit to fill her. And as that happens, give her opportunities to embrace others with God-given love, joy, peace, patience, kindness, goodness, faithful, gentleness, and self-control (Galatians 5:22-23). Amen.

One More Peek

Therefore, as God's chosen people, holy and dearly loved, clothe yourselves with compassion, kindness, humility, gentleness and patience (Colossians 3:12).

Detours

Because of the LORD's great love we are not consumed,
for his compassions never fail.
They are new every morning;
great is your faithfulness.

LAMENTATIONS 3:22-23

Upward Gaze

Father, I praise You because You are a faithful God who does no wrong (Deuteronomy 32:4). Your Word is upright and true. You are faithful in all You do. You love righteousness and justice; the earth is full of Your unfailing love (Psalm 33:4-5). Thank You, God!

❧

Picture this: We're cruising through life, enjoying sunshine and scenery along Easy Street. The journey's great, despite a few bumps. But one fine day, we crest a steep hill and everything changes.

Screeeeeech! A flashing orange arrow blocks the road and directs us down an unfamiliar route, one that hugs a mountainside. A rock wall shoots straight up on our right. A sheer cliff drops to our left. There's no escape. The only way out is through.

Sound familiar?

If circumstances beyond your control have interrupted your journey with a white-knuckle detour, be encouraged. You're not alone. Every minute of every day, women travel roads they don't choose. Divorce, illness, and accidents propel us into unfamiliar territory.

Our family experienced a life-altering detour upon our second child's birth. We'd worked in Nepal for nearly three years when Stephanie was born with hydrocephalus—too much water on the brain.

In the weeks prior, we'd committed our lives to the Nepalese people. We'd made plans to complete our original commitment with our short-term agency and then switch to a career agency. But on March 19, 1985, everything changed. An imaginary flashing orange arrow directed us down a real, unfamiliar, and frightening route.

Hydrocephalus threatened our newborn's life. Without a shunt to drain the excess fluid, she would die. Phone calls flew between the hospital compound, our agency's headquarters in Kathmandu, and a travel agent. Within 72 hours, Gene and Stephanie boarded a plane and headed for Seattle.

The airline refused to let me fly. "You've just had a Caesarean section. You're considered high risk," the agent said. "Wait five days for the next flight."

Left behind with my 20-month-old son and my mother-in-law (the dear woman arrived two days prior to Steph's birth), I lay on my bed and cried hot tears. *Will my baby live? Will I see her again?* Circumstances nearly overwhelmed me. Besides facing our newborn's uncertain future, we were returning to the States with nothing—no home, no job, no car, no health insurance.

I careened down a road that hugged a mountainside. A rock wall shot straight up on one side; a sheer cliff threatened me on the other. There was no escape, no turning back. But in those dark days, I discovered I wasn't traveling that road alone. As the tears coursed down my cheeks, a still small voice whispered peace:

"Great is Thy faithfulness, O God my Father,
There is no shadow of turning with Thee;
Thou changest not, Thy compassions, they fail not,
As Thou has been Thou forever wilt be.*

The lyrics washed fear from my thoughts. Our journey had suddenly changed, but God hadn't. He knew my fears, and in the midst of them, He promised to be the same as always—faithful.

Detours happen. Sometimes they're massive, like 9/11. That morning, thousands careened down an unfamiliar road as widows, widowers, or single parents. Most often, detours happen in a smaller scale but equally life-altering way. Perhaps a spouse suffers a stroke or heart attack. A house fire destroys our belongings. A job transfer uproots us from everything familiar. A teenage daughter announces she's pregnant. Cancer strikes.

Detours change our direction. They propel us onto a route we didn't choose. We can easily grow angry or bitter. We might blame God or vent frustration on other people, especially if their choices initiated the detour. But if we respond negatively, we miss the opportunity to enjoy fellowship with God, our constant travel companion.

The next time a detour redirects us, we can remember that although our circumstances have changed, God's faithfulness remains the same. He doesn't expect us to travel the road alone. He knows our fears and anxieties, and He's able to calm them when we cry out to Him. Rather than regarding detours as threats, we can view them as opportunities to develop a more intimate relationship with Him as He travels with us.

Inward Glimpse

Dear Father, thank You that although my circumstances change, You remain faithful. Help me turn to You rather than worry when I encounter a detour. Amen.

- Read the hymn "Great Is Thy Faithfulness." What do the lyrics teach us about God's faithfulness?

---

* Words by Thomas O. Chisholm. Copyright 1923. Renewal 1951. Hope Publishing Company, Carol Stream, Illinois. All rights reserved. Used by permission.

- What unexpected detours have you faced? How has the Lord met you there?

Outward Glance

Father, if _____'s life takes a detour, teach her to be anxious for nothing but to bring all her concerns to You in prayer and with thanksgiving. In those times, fill her with Your peace that passes all understanding. Guard her heart and mind in Christ Jesus (Philippians 4:6-7). Amen.

One More Peek

But the Lord is faithful, and he will strengthen and protect you from the evil one (2 Thessalonians 3:3).

Great Is Thy Faithfulness

Thomas O. Chisholm

Great is Thy faithfulness, O God my Father,
There is no shadow of turning with Thee;
Thou changest not, Thy compassions, they fail not;
As Thou hast been Thou forever wilt be.

Summer and winter, and springtime and harvest,
Sun, moon, and stars in their courses above,
Join with all nature in manifold witness
To Thy great faithfulness, mercy, and love.

Pardon for sin and a peace that endureth,
Thine own dear presence to cheer and to guide;
Strength for today and bright hope for tomorrow,
Blessings all mine, with ten thousand beside!

Great is Thy faithfulness! Great is Thy faithfulness!
Morning by morning new mercies I see;
All I have needed Thy hand hath provided—
Great is Thy faithfulness, Lord, unto me!*

Comfort

As a mother comforts her child,
so will I comfort you.

ISAIAH 66:13

Upward Gaze

Father, I praise You for being the Father of compassion and God of all comfort. You comfort us in all our troubles, and through Christ our comfort overflows (2 Corinthians 1:3-5). Amen.

~

Sharon sat at her parents' kitchen table and silently watched her mother feed her father. *The last lunch together in their own home,* she thought. *I knew this day would come, but I never dreamed it would hurt so much.*

Several years earlier, Alzheimer's had begun to take possession of her dad's body and mind. Her mother had assumed caregiving responsibilities. But as the disease progressed, her father became physically aggressive. With her mother's well-being at risk, the family decided to place her father in a nursing home. Today was the day.

Sharon pushed her salad around her plate. *Does Dad recognize me? After their 47-year marriage, does he know his wife? Does he understand what's happening today? Does he feel the same pain we feel?*

She cleared the dirty dishes as her mom turned on the television and settled her father in a chair beside a window. Before long, she realized her mother had disappeared. She found her in the bathroom, sobbing. Without saying a word, the two women embraced and cried together.

"Mom, we're in no shape to leave yet," said Sharon. "Let's sit down for a few minutes." She led her mom to the room where the television screen flashed unwatched images. A Christian program caught her attention as she flipped through the TV channels.

On the show, a couple recalled their recent car accident that killed one of their children. The husband had sustained serious injuries and undergone extensive therapy. His health would likely never return to normal. Despite their grief, the couple acknowledged God's greatness and recalled the ways in which He'd helped them through their ordeal.

Sharon listened intently. The couple's tragic yet triumphant testimony encouraged her. *If those people can survive their circumstances, we can survive ours*, she thought. She sensed the Lord wrapping His arms around her and her mother through the couple's words, sending them comfort when they needed it most.

That's so like God! He knows our concerns. He feels our pain. When we hurt, He hurts. And He sends comfort at just the right moment.

A mother's response to her child aptly demonstrates the same thing. The other day, I saw a youngster riding his bike minus the training wheels. He teetered and swerved, and then he crashed into a curb and fell to the road. He scraped his knee, scratched his palms, and came up crying.

The boy's mother was riding her bike behind him. When she saw the accident, she immediately rushed to her child's rescue. She knelt beside him, examined his injury, wiped his tears, and gave him a big hug. She wouldn't have considered biking past her child, belittling his pain or shouting, "Get over it!"

Sooner or later we all experience pain. A job transfer sends a dear friend to the far side of nowhere. A child leaves home for college. A spouse betrays us. A disabling disease progresses. The cause differs, but the effect is the same—we hurt. Like the child who crashed his bike, we only need to cry out, and our heavenly Father rushes to our rescue.

Sometimes God comforts us through a testimony, as He did in Sharon's case. We hear another's story and realize that we too can survive our trial. Sometimes He hugs us through a Scripture promise or through song lyrics that soothe the pain. Sometimes He touches our point of need through a pastor's sermon or a child's kiss.

God's methods of comforting us are as infinite as He is. But regardless of His method, He desires one thing—that His comfort fills our hearts, overflows, and spills into the lives of hurting individuals around us. That's what happened when the couple on television told their testimony—Sharon heard their account and found comfort.

May we find comfort in time of need, and may our lives bless others in the same way.

Inward Glimpse

Dear Father, thank You for being the God of all comfort. Keep my heart sensitive to those experiencing pain so they too might know Your comfort through me. Amen.

- Recall a situation in which God ran to your rescue and comforted you. How did He do that?
- Ask God to open your eyes to recognize when someone needs comfort.

Outward Glance

Father, I pray that _____ will find comfort in Your Word and in Your unfailing love (Psalm 119:52,76). And when she experiences Your comfort, may it overflow and spill into the lives of those around her. Amen.

One More Peek

Remember your word to your servant,
for you have given me hope.
My comfort in my suffering is this:
Your promise preserves my life (Psalm 119:49-50).

Beware the Danger!

"Martha, Martha," the Lord answered, "you are worried and upset about many things, but only one thing is needed. Mary has chosen what is better, and it will not be taken away from her."

LUKE 10:41

Upward Gaze

Father, in the midst of life's pressures and responsibilities, I lift my eyes to You, the one whose throne is in heaven (Psalm 123:1). I know my help comes from You—the Maker of heaven and earth (Psalm 121:2). That knowledge fills me with strength and hope. Praise You!

~

Monday morning arrived with a to-do list that grew longer by the minute. I watered my outdoor plants and swept the deck, pausing only to watch the hummingbirds sip the last drops of sweet syrup from the feeder. *I'll mix another batch,* I thought. I poured a cup of water into a saucepan, added ¼ cup sugar, and turned on the stove's front element. *While this heats, I'll make a phone call.*

I phoned from my office, down the hall from the kitchen. By doing so, I could chat and file papers at the same time. All was well—until a smoke detector's shrill warning nearly split my eardrums.

"What in the world...?" I said. "Could you hold for a moment? My smoke detector has a problem." I ran to the kitchen, stopped, and stared!

I'd completely forgotten about the hummingbird juice heating on the stove! Grey smoke hid the kitchen ceiling and billowed through the living room. The stove element glowed red. My hummingbird juice had morphed into black sponge-like goo.

I raced back to the phone. "Gotta go! Call ya later!" I ran around the house opening doors and windows, giving thanks that our house still had doors and windows to open.

The situation served as a wake-up call: In my busyness, I'd accidentally created a potentially dangerous situation.

Is it possible that we do the same thing in our spiritual lives?

As women, we spend countless hours each week driving kids to extracurriculars, helping aging parents, fulfilling work responsibilities, volunteering at school or church, and keeping our families fed and clothed. Like the hummingbirds, we zip from one activity to the next. But constant activity breeds potential danger: We're left with little time to ponder eternal truths and safeguard our spiritual lives.

We don't intentionally neglect Bible reading—it just happens. We don't deliberately choose not to pray. It's just that...well, life gets hectic sometimes. Before long, we lose our sensitivity to the Holy Spirit's gentle nudges. We find temptations more tempting. We begin to rationalize sin. Our spiritual lives may be in danger, but we're too busy to see it. How can we guard against that?

For starters, we can carve time into our schedules for reading God's Word. Doing so may require getting up 20 minutes earlier or reading during our lunch break, but the benefit is worth the effort. Personally, my Bible reading doesn't happen if I don't do it before my day's activities begin. Once I begin writing, running errands, or doing housework, it's nearly impossible for me to stop, slow my thoughts, and focus on God's Word.

We can find an accountability partner. Sharing new insights with a friend on a regular basis can provide the incentive we need to keep Bible reading and prayer consistent.

We can fill our minds with God's thoughts by memorizing Scripture or by writing Bible promises on 3 x 5 cards and posting them where we'll see them often—by the kitchen sink, on the bathroom mirror, on the computer, or on the dashboard of the car.

We can practice God's presence by conversing with Him throughout our day and as we fall asleep at night. And we can evaluate and prioritize our activities—do they yield temporal or eternal results?

To-do lists can rule our lives if we let them. But let's make sure that cultivating our spiritual lives remains number one on those lists! We'll experience increased sensitivity to the Holy Spirit's voice as He tells us how to live and what to say. Peace and joy will replace worry and fear. And we'll become women who reflect joy and strength far beyond our own.

Inward Glimpse

Dear Father, thank You for showing me that I must safeguard my spiritual development. Make me alert to those things that could endanger my relationship with You. Amen.

- What spiritual disciplines need a little boost in your life?
- Write a meaningful Scripture verse on a 3 x 5 card and post it where you'll see if often. Leave it there for a week and then replace it with another. Repeat!

Outward Glance

Father, I pray that _____ will regard her relationship with You as top priority. May she open her mouth wide and pant for Your commandments. Turn to her and have mercy on her. Direct her footsteps according to Your Word and do not let any sin rule over her (Psalm 119:131-133). Thank You. Amen.

One More Peek

Still others, like seed sown among thorns, hear the word; but the worries of this life, the deceitfulness of wealth and the desires for other things come in and choke the word, making it unfruitful (Mark 4:18-19).

Enjoy the Ride

Be still, and know that I am God;
I will be exalted among the nations,
I will be exalted in the earth.

Upward Gaze

I will shout joyfully to You, Lord, and I will serve You with gladness. I come before You with joyful songs because You are God! You made me, and I am a sheep in Your pasture. I enter Your gates with thanksgiving and Your courts with praise. Bless Your name, for You are good. Your love and faithfulness will reign through all generations (Psalm 100). Amen.

~

"What do you say?" Gene asked. His eyes twinkled. "Do you want to make it a family vacation?"

"Sounds great to me!" I said. "Let's do it!"

Gene was scheduled to attend a weeklong convention in San Diego, and he wanted us to accompany him. While he attended daily meetings, the kids and I would hang out by the hotel pool. We'd spend evenings sightseeing and then visit the zoo and Sea World on the weekend.

Departure day arrived. Late Friday afternoon, Gene rolled into the driveway with a borrowed RV not much bigger than a kid's overgrown toy. We crammed clothes, swimsuits, and beach towels into every empty cupboard. We stocked the fridge with juice and snacks. We packed coloring books, crayons, squirt guns, bubble bottles, and gizmos and gadgets of every possible description to entertain the kids. We waved to the neighbors, shouted "San Diego or bust!" and rumbled off the driveway toward our destination.

I wish I could say that the trip began as smooth as melted ice cream on a hot summer day, but to do that, I'd have to lie. Five minutes after locking the house and heading to the highway, we stopped at a bank to get some cash. That's when it happened.

"Are we almost there?" peeped a pip-squeak voice.

Gene and I stared at each other in disbelief and then burst into laughter. We were five minutes from home. *Five minutes.* Only 16 hours remained!

A few minutes later, another little voice declared, "She's in my space!" Then came "I'm hot!" and "I'm thirsty!" and "I have to go potty." Finally, "I'm tired of driving." Thirty minutes into the trip we stopped for dinner, with only 15½ hours left. If the kids continued this behavior, we'd be staring at one very, very l-o-n-g drive.

Thankfully, the atmosphere changed after dinner. The kids grew tired, so they put on their pajamas and crawled into bed. The vehicle's constant motion lulled them to sleep within a few miles.

Gene and I looked at each other once more. This time we heaved twin sighs of relief. Peace and quiet filled the camper as our mini-passengers slept. We drove through the night toward our destination while they rested, relaxed and worry-free.

As believers, we're like passengers traveling through this world en route to a special destination. Sometimes, like our kids, we whine a little. Sometimes a lot—"The weather's lousy." "I want a bigger house." "I want more money." "I don't like my job." "She's in my space." We grow distracted and irritated. We forget that the trip is only temporary and that heaven awaits.

Whining stops when we learn to rest in our heavenly Father's care. He has planned every detail of our journey. He knows the way. He knows how long it will take. And He knows that our destination will bring untold delight. He wants us to trust His promises and enjoy His companionship.

When we're tempted to whine, we can choose to give thanks and praise instead. By doing so, we'll find our trip more enjoyable, and guess what? So will those around us!

Inward Glimpse

Heavenly Father, I'm so glad You've planned my journey. Help me rest along the way. Amen.

- On a scale of one to ten, with ten being fantastic, what's your ability to rest along your journey? Fill in the blank with as many answers as you can: "I will trust God for _____."

- Write a prayer expressing your thankfulness to the Lord for planning every mile of your journey. Ask Him to help you rest along the way!

Outward Glance

Father, I pray that _____ will delight herself in You and that You will grant her the desires of her heart. May she commit her way to You and trust You for wisdom, strength, safety, and health. As she trusts in You, please perform Your good plan. Bring forth her righteousness as the light. Make the justice of her cause like the noonday sun. Teach her to rest in You and to wait patiently for You to accomplish Your desires (Psalm 37:4-7). Amen.

One More Peek

Find rest, O my soul, in God alone;
    my hope comes from him (Psalm 62:5).

Fresh and Fruitful

His delight is in the law of the LORD,
and on his law he meditates day and night.
He is like a tree planted by streams of water,
which yields it fruit in season
and whose leaf does not wither.
Whatever he does prospers.

PSALM 1:2-3

Upward Gaze

Father, I praise You for being trustworthy and for blessing those who place their confidence in You (Psalm 40:4). Thank You for telling me how to live a life that resembles a strong, fruitful tree. I delight to obey and wait for You to fulfill Your promises. Amen.

~

Summer heat pushed the thermometer's mercury to 97 degrees in the shade. Bev's potted pansies browned and drooped. *My flowers look like I feel,* she thought. *Wilted and weary.*

She recalled the past year's events: First, her husband lost his job one month before their oldest child left home for college. Financial issues and releasing her son had produced more stress than she'd anticipated. Two months later, her widowed mom suffered a crippling stroke. Bev had no siblings, so she'd moved her mom into their home and assumed responsibility for her care. That meant tending to her mom's round-the-clock needs while parenting two teenagers, maintaining her marriage, and running a household.

Bev's Bible reading, once regular, no longer existed. Her running conversations with God had fallen by the wayside, replaced by constant worry. Her inner joy had dried up long ago. And peace? She'd forgotten its meaning.

Bev filled a watering can and poured its contents into the flower pots. She turned on the radio and plopped into a chair to sip iced tea. She caught the final strains of a popular worship song, and then the announcer introduced a Christian speaker. His first words nearly knocked her off her chair. "Have you ever felt wilted and weary? Would you like to know the secret to spiritual vitality?"

The speaker continued, explaining Jeremiah 17:7-8. "God blesses those who place their confidence in Him," he said. "They become like a tree firmly planted by a stream. This tree has no fear when heat comes. It has no worries in times of drought. It constantly produces green leaves and fruit.

"If we want to be like this tree, we must make our relationship with Jesus Christ our number one priority. We must rely on His strength and wisdom, not our own, in whatever situations we face. He'll sustain us despite the heat of life's demands and trials."

The words resonated with Bev. *That's it! I've let my relationship with the Lord slip. By doing so, I've placed my confidence in…me.*

Father, forgive me, she prayed. *Help me keep my relationship with You as my number one priority. Guard me from thinking I can handle life on my own.*

We're sometimes prone to trust in our own understanding or strength from day to day. We might manage awhile, but eventually our resources prove insufficient. Physical, emotional, mental, and spiritual weariness sets in.

Sometimes we place our confidence in tangible things—a beautiful home, a dream job, an impressive resume, a healthy marriage, a hearty bank account. We think their presence will meet our needs. The problem is, they can disappear in an instant. Then what?

The secret to spiritual vitality lies not in ourselves or in things but in knowing the person and promises of God. When we spend regular time in His Word, fill our minds with Scripture, and learn to practice His presence moment by moment, the heat won't affect us.

Friendship with God gives us the strength to survive and thrive despite busyness and less than desirable circumstances. When the heat rises, we can resemble strong, healthy trees—fresh and fruitful—rather than Bev's wilted, weary pansies.

Inward Glimpse

Dear Father, thank You for giving me the power to live as a fresh, fruitful tree. Help me trust in You alone. Amen.

- If you're feeling wilted and weary, fill your home with praise and worship music. Ask the Holy Spirit to show you how to change, and purpose to do what He says.

- Memorize Jeremiah 17:7—"But blessed is the man who trusts in the LORD, whose confidence is in him."

Outward Glance

Father, I pray that _____ will flourish like a palm tree and grow like a cedar of Lebanon. Bless her with fruit-bearing, even in old age. And open her mouth to proclaim the truth about Your character (Psalm 92:12-15). Amen.

One More Peek

Trust in him at all times, O people;
pour out your hearts to him,
for God is our refuge (Psalm 62:8).

Embracing Change

Every good and perfect gift is from above,
coming down from the Father of the heavenly lights,
who does not change like shifting shadows.

JAMES 1:17

Upward Gaze

Father, You are a refuge for the poor and the needy in distress. You're a shelter from the storm and a shade from the heat (Isaiah 25:4). You're an eternal Rock—unmovable in the midst of change (Isaiah 26:4). In You I trust. Amen.

~

Natasha checked her e-mail for the third time in one hour. *Maybe this time I'll have a message from someone back home,* she thought. She caught herself. *When will I stop calling California "home"?*

Her computer's Inbox contained nothing new, so she poured herself a cup of coffee, threw another log on the fire, and curled up in her favorite chair. She gazed out the window at the swirling snow and shivered. Four months had passed since her husband's transfer to Alaska.

Relocating had brought a host of changes—some easy, some difficult. Natasha made a mental list of some changes they'd made: family doctor, piano teacher, hairdresser, dentist, school, friends, bank....

A tear rolled down Natasha's cheek as she thought of her best girl-friend in California. They'd lived only one block apart. They took turns driving the kids to school and sipped lattés together at least two mornings each week. *Will I find a close friend here?* she wondered.

Moving also meant quitting her job. Natasha had assisted a florist for weddings and other special events. She loved the variety and flexible hours. She'd looked for similar employment in her new town but found nothing so far.

Leaving the church her family had attended for 12 years was the most difficult change. Natasha and her husband had enjoyed a closer relationship with the congregation than with their extended families, whom they seldom saw. Since the move, they'd visited several congregations but hadn't found one that grabbed them. A sense of isolation swept over her.

If I'd known this change would be so difficult, I might not have had the courage to make it, Natasha thought.

I can relate. We've moved nine times in 23 years...and that's nothing compared to military families. Some of our moves took us halfway around the world. We left familiarity behind, adjusted to a different climate, learned a new language and culture, and ate different food. Returning to North America meant doing it again in reverse.

I thought moving from Washington to British Columbia would be much simpler. Wrong. I wrestled with loneliness for three years. I missed my house. I missed my friends. I missed my church family. I missed the life we'd grown to love.

Thankfully, things improved. Besides establishing new friendships and finding a wonderful home church, my prayer life deepened, and I began to write. But in the darkness before dawn, I often had the same thought Natasha did: *If I'd known this change would be so difficult, I might not have had the courage to make it.*

Change is inevitable. It happens every day. It wears many faces. Marriage—we adapt our lifestyle to blend with our mate's. Parenthood—we're suddenly responsible to meet the needs of helpless little people. Then they grow up and leave home, and we have to adjust to an empty nest.

What other changes do we experience? Beginning a new job. Losing a spouse. Welcoming a new pastor. Inaugurating a new president. Sometimes change happens slowly; sometimes in an instant. Sometimes we welcome change. Other times...well, we wonder if we'll survive.

Regardless of the changes we encounter in our lifetime, we can face them with courage. Why? Because the God who never changes holds us in His hands. He knows our needs and is more than able to meet them. When we understand God's sovereignty over our lives, we can embrace change as a tool by which we get to know Him more intimately. We can view it as an opportunity to experience His strength, His provision, His wisdom. And when we do, we'll discover than we'll not only survive...we'll thrive!

Inward Glimpse

Dear Father, thank You for being sovereign in my life. Help me view changes as opportunities to know You more intimately. Amen.

- What changes have you experienced in the last year? How has God met you in those changes?
- Read the hymn "Be Still My Soul." What stanza means the most to you and why?

Outward Glance

Father, when _____ faces change, may she find You to be her strong confidence. Keep her foot from being caught in fear or self-pity (Proverbs 3:26). Rather, keep her mind on You and grant her peace (Isaiah 26:3). Amen.

One More Peek

Jesus Christ is the same yesterday and today and forever (Hebrews 13:8).

Be Still, My Soul

Katharina von Schlegel
translated by Jane L. Borthwick

Be still, my soul: the Lord is on thy side;
Bear patiently the cross of grief or pain;
Leave to thy God to order and provide;
In every change He faithful will remain.
Be still, my soul: thy best, thy heav'nly Friend
Thro' thorny ways leads to a joyful end.

Be still, my soul: thy God doth undertake
To guide the future as He has the past.
Thy hope, thy confidence let nothing shake;
All now mysterious shall be bright at last.
Be still, my soul: the waves and winds still know
His voice who ruled them while He dwelt below.

Be still, my soul: the hour is hast'ning on
When we shall be forever with the Lord,
When disappointment, grief, and fear are gone,
Sorrow forgot, love's purest joys restored.
Be still, my soul: when change and tears are past,
All safe and blessed we shall meet at last.

Laced Punch

Buy the truth and do not sell it;
get wisdom, discipline and understanding.

PROVERBS 23:23

Upward Gaze

Father, troubles sometimes surround me. When my sins overtake me, I cannot see. But in my sorrow, You send Your mercy. Your love and truth protect me (Psalm 40:11). Into Your hands I commit my spirit, O God of truth (Psalm 31:5). Amen.

~

Stop! Before you read this story, you need some background information: My Mennonite upbringing instructed me to avoid certain taboos—card playing, dancing, smoking, attending movies, and drinking alcohol. I obeyed for the most part. I did intentionally sniff some beer once, but that was my closest association with the stuff.

After we married, Gene and I spent nearly 12 years in Washington while he worked for an engineering firm. The office held social get-togethers each Friday. The employees were offered munchies, soft drinks, and *other* drinks. Let me be specific. By *other* drinks, I mean alcohol-laced punch. Not enough to make anyone tipsy, mind you, or so the food coordinator thought. Enough background. On with the story...

I swung my car into the firm's parking lot on a drizzly Friday afternoon. Gene and I were Seattle-bound for a romantic weekend getaway to celebrate our tenth wedding anniversary. I arrived as the office get-together ended.

The employees said their goodbyes and filtered out. Gene had one more thing to do before leaving, so I waited in the common room. That's when I saw the punch bowl. I never considered that it might contain more than fruit juice and ginger ale.

Hmmm, I thought. *Looks good. There's a lot left over. Surely no one would mind if I helped myself.* I poured myself one glass of the tropical drink. The liquid warmed my esophagus on its way down. *That's odd*, I thought. Call me naïve or just plain stupid—I poured myself another glass and tried again. This time I thought it smelled a little "off," but I downed it anyway. I was thirsty, after all.

Gene returned and we hopped in our car. Several miles down the road, however, strange things started happening. Road signs appeared blurry. They slid backward and forward. Oncoming cars careened toward us and then away.

"Something's wrong with my eyes," I said. "Everything's moving."

Gene cast me a sideways glance. "Are you okay?"

I cocked my head and giggled. "Whadaya mean?"

He looked at me in disbelief. "Oh, my goodness! I never thought I'd see this day." He stifled his laughter. "You drank the punch, didn't you? Someone added an extra something-or-other to it. That's explains why you can't see straight!"

Up until now, only three or four people on the face of this earth have heard this story. Frankly, it's a little embarrassing. But I'm disclosing my secret because it teaches an important object lesson for our spiritual lives. Stay with me!

Throughout Scripture, we read that God's word is truth. He promises blessings to those who believe and obey His law. Psalm 19:8 says, "The precepts of the LORD are right, giving joy to the heart. The commands of the LORD are radiant, giving light to the eyes." Another version calls the Lord's commands "pure." When we let the Bible—pure truth—satisfy our spiritual thirst, we find joy, wisdom, and peace. We find life itself.

Sadly, sometimes we think the Bible needs additional pizzazz. We want our emotional and spiritual taste buds tingled. Like lacing pure tropical punch, we mix truth with a dash of human logic. *God says He hates divorce, but my husband's a dud, and I'm attracted to someone else. Surely He wouldn't want me to be unhappy by staying in my marriage.*

We add a splash of society's standards. *I'm a valuable woman only if my dress size is 12 or less.*

We toss in a dose of scientific rationale. *Who would place their faith in a God they can't see?*

We drink deeply, and before long, we're intoxicated by something other than God's proven recipe for life. The result? Our spiritual vision blurs. We confuse right and wrong. We make poor choices that sometimes carry lifelong consequences.

If we want to make a difference in our families, churches, and communities, let's quench our spiritual thirst with God's pure Word rather than the world's laced punch. We can ask the Holy Spirit to teach us discernment, and He'll help us recognize when someone's added an extra something-or-other.

Inward Glimpse

Dear Father, thank You for giving me Your pure Word. Guard me from altering its truth by mixing it with error. Amen.

- Have you mixed the truth of God's Word with human philosophy in any way? If so, what are the specifics?
- Memorize Psalm 19:8 (it's included in today's reading).

Outward Glance

Father, I pray that _____ will choose the way of truth. May she set her heart on Your laws (Psalm 119:30). Teach her to embrace the pure fear of the Lord. Help her remember that Your ordinances are sure and totally righteous, and that You reward those who obey them (Psalm 19:9,11). Amen.

One More Peek

They exchanged the truth of God for a lie, and worshiped and served created things rather than the Creator—who is forever praised. Amen (Romans 1:25).

Unshakable Joy

Let the heavens rejoice, let the earth be glad;
let them say among the nations, "The LORD reigns!"

1 CHRONICLES 16:31

Upward Gaze

Father, You're worthy of praise because splendor and majesty are before You. Strength and joy are in Your dwelling place (1 Chronicles 16:27). Let the sea and its contents resound. Let the fields and their contents be jubilant. Let the trees of the forest sing for joy, for You come to judge the earth. I thank You, Lord, for You are good. Your love endures forever (1 Chronicles 16:32-34). Amen.

~

I swung our car into the school's parking lot and glanced at my watch. "Hurry!" I urged my daughters, drumming my fingers on the steering wheel. "I'm late for my appointment!"

"Have a good day, Mom," called Stephanie as she jumped out. "Don't forget to smile." I faked a goofy grin. She rolled her eyes and dashed off.

Don't forget to smile. I needed that reminder. The day had dawned full of cheer, but things weren't feeling chipper anymore. Let me explain…

Living on an island means our lives revolve around ferry schedules. When the ferry runs late, plans fall like dominoes. This particular morning, the 8:00 A.M. ferry departed for town 15 minutes late. As a result, the girls missed their connecting ride on the other side. Luckily I was there and could drive them to school, but doing so meant I'd be late for my 8:30 mammogram appointment. And that would make me late for two meetings scheduled after the X-ray.

"Have a good day. Don't forget to smile." Yeah, right.

I watched the girls disappear through the school's front door and felt guilty for contaminating their day with my sourpuss outlook. *God, forgive me. Please overhaul my attitude,* I prayed.

When I arrived at the hospital's X-ray department, the technician greeted me pleasantly. "Sorry I'm late," I said. "No problem," she replied. She performed her task efficiently, and within minutes I was en route to the next appointment. By noon I'd completed my activities—on time—and was parked in the ferry terminal's line for my return trip home.

The wait provided opportunity for quiet contemplation: Why had minor unforeseen circumstances frustrated me so? Why had I allowed a simple schedule glitch to influence my attitude and affect those I loved the most?

When I arrived home, I opened my Bible for a spiritual refresher. Today's key verse leaped off the page—"Let the heavens rejoice, let the earth be glad; let them say among the nations, 'The LORD reigns!'"

True joy has nothing to do with changing circumstances! I thought. *It's based on the fact that the Lord reigns!*

That's so true, isn't it? In a blink, circumstances can change from bright to bleak. When that happens, joy isn't the normal by-product. For instance, what emotion do we feel when rain ruins our family's much anticipated camping trip, or someone dents our car, or an airline loses our luggage?

As I said, joy isn't the norm. But God has given us everything we need to respond supernaturally to life's little bumps. By memorizing and meditating on His Word, we can face frustrations with a positive outlook. Rather than nursing a bad attitude, we can say, "The Lord reigns!" and ask Him to resolve the situation in a way that honors Him.

So, dear reader, go ahead. Have a good day. Remember that God loves you. Remember that He's in control of all things and that His faithfulness never ends. And don't forget to smile!

Inward Glimpse

Dear Father, thank You for being my source of joy. Keep my focus on You when circumstances shift. Amen.

• Describe an instance when God filled your heart with joy in the midst of a difficult time. What particular thought or Bible verse helped you through it?

• Memorize Psalm 16:11 from today's "One More Peek."

Outward Glance

Father, I pray that _____ will find Your strength to be her joy (Nehemiah 8:10). Hear her when she cries to You. Be merciful to her, be her helper. And when You turn her wailing into dancing and clothe her with joy, may her heart sing to You. May she give thanks to You forever (Psalm 30:10-12). Amen.

One More Peek

You have made known to me the path of life;
  you will fill me with joy in your presence,
    with eternal pleasures at your right hand (Psalm 16:11).

True Love

Dear children, let us not love with words or tongue
but with actions and in truth.

1 JOHN 3:18

Upward Gaze

God, Your Word says that You showed Your love for me in
this: While I was still a sinner, Christ died for me (Romans
5:8). I praise You for not only telling me that You love me
but also demonstrating it with actions. Amen.

~

Kathleen analyzed her reflection in the bathroom mirror. She lifted
a few strands of hair. *Short,* she thought. *I want it short, but I don't want
to pay twenty-five dollars. I'll bet I could do this myself.* She grabbed a
pair of scissors and began snipping.

My friend is neither a cheapskate nor too poor to afford a haircut.
Rather, she's a warmhearted people lover and a follower of Jesus Christ.
And that's what motivated her to start cutting...

71

Several months earlier, Kathleen had received a letter from Esther, a Christian woman in India. She'd read an article that Kathleen had written and wondered if she was a believer. A long-distance friendship blossomed between the two. They exchanged photos of home and family.

Esther revealed that she belonged to the Dalit caste—India's untouchables. Nevertheless, she'd earned a master's degree in English literature. She taught for several years and then quit and started an orphanage in her home. That grew into a 40-bed boys' facility and a tailoring school to teach young women a trade. She then began helping 100 destitute women—widows, abandoned wives, and victims of bride burnings—by providing them with physical resources and moral and spiritual support. "Come to India and see what God is doing," she urged Kathleen.

At first, Kathleen listed the obstacles: too hot, too many creepy critters, too expensive. But when she wrote an article that netted the exact income as her initial expenses, she stopped arguing and began making travel plans.

Several weeks before she left home, Kathleen phoned Esther. "I'd like to bring a small gift for each woman, and something for the boys. Any suggestions?"

"Well, the children need pencils and pens. And most of the women need new saris but can't afford them. You can buy them here for five dollars apiece."

Kathleen nearly choked when she did the mental math. Where would she find $500? Several days after that conversation, she cut her own hair. She'd saved $25—a mere shadow of the $500 she needed. But hey, the savings purchased five saris!

Everywhere she went, people commented on her inch-long hair. When she told them about Esther and explained why it was so short ("Oops, now it's longer on the right side. I'd best trim it up. Uh-oh, now it's longer on the left..."), they laughed and joined her cause. Before long, she had $1500! The money paid for pillows and blankets for 40 boys and saris for a hundred women whose gratitude charged the room when the garments were distributed.

"We must convert our love for Christ into deeds. We must express Christian love in concrete, living ways," said Mother Teresa, who ministered to India's poorest of the poor. Compared to her legacy, we may feel our deeds are so insignificant that they'll never make a dent. And if that's the case, why bother?

We can remember that our deeds needn't be big if they're rooted in love for Christ. Scripture tells the story of a widow who visited the temple treasury. While others donated large amounts of money, this woman contributed two small copper coins, worth only a fraction of a penny.

How did Jesus respond? Recognizing that she gave from a heart rooted in love for God, He looked beyond the coins' monetary value and taught that her deed was greater than the huge financial sums the rich folks gave (Mark 12:41-44).

We might not have the opportunity to convert our love for Christ into a ministry like Mother Teresa's or even into a five-sari haircut that snowballs into a shopping spree. But we can listen to a child read, or write an encouraging note to his teacher. When we use our husband's car, we can fill up the gas tank. We can grocery shop for a shut-in or spend time teaching our teen to drive (minus gasps and high-pitched commands).

If we say we love Christ but don't communicate it through our actions, our words mean nothing. Let's look for opportunities to convert our love for Christ into deeds. Remember—words plus deeds equal changed lives.

Inward Glimpse

Dear Father, thank You for loving me not only through words but through Your actions. Help me do the same for others. Amen.

- Think of someone who is difficult to love. Now think of one thing you can do to demonstrate love. You have to follow through or it doesn't count!

- Write an encouragement note or send a greeting card to a shut-in.

Outward Glance

Father, I pray that _____'s faith and actions will work together and that her faith will be made complete by what she does (James 2:22). May her deeds, regardless of how small or large, reveal her profession of love for You. Amen.

One More Peek

As the body without the spirit is dead, so faith without deeds is dead (James 2:26).

Hannah's Worship

*Therefore, I urge you, brothers, in view of God's mercy,
to offer your bodies as living sacrifices, holy
and pleasing to God—which is your spiritual worship.*

ROMANS 12:1

Upward Gaze

Father God, You are worthy of praise, honor, glory, and power now and forever. There is no one like You, the Rock (1 Samuel 2:2). You alone work wonders. You alone are majestic in holiness, awesome in glory (Exodus 15:11). Praise You!

~

What is worship? In his book *The Purpose-Driven Life*, Rick Warren writes, "Anthropologists have noted that worship is a universal urge, hard-wired by God into the very fiber of our being—an inbuilt need to connect with God." He says that depending on our religious background, some folks might equate it with singing, praying, lighting ceremonial candles, or celebrating communion. But worship is much broader than performing these religious acts.

True worship is a lifestyle that brings God pleasure. At its heart lies surrender—total, unconditional surrender to God's sovereign plan. The Bible teems with stories about ordinary people whose lives exemplify true worship. Take Hannah, for instance.

Beautiful, barren Hannah knelt alone before the Lord. Tears coursed down her cheeks as she thought about her husband, Elkanah, and his other wife, Peninnah.

Elkanah loves me. I see it in his eyes. I hear it in his voice. I feel it in his touch. But his love can't erase the pain Peninnah's ridicule brings. A sob escaped her lips as she recalled Peninnah's jeers: "God has blessed me with children. Why hasn't He blessed you?"

Hannah's lips moved silently, expressing a passionate plea. *Almighty God, give me a son. If You do, I'll give him back to You. He'll be Yours for service for the rest of his life. I beg You, grant me a son.*

Within a year, Peninnah's contempt fell silent. Hannah held her newborn son, Samuel, to her breast and gazed at his face. She stroked his silky head and inhaled his baby-fresh sweetness.

When the day arrived for Hannah to fulfill her promise, she delivered Samuel to Eli, the temple priest. She settled him into his new home and turned to leave. What emotions did she feel at that moment? Did she regret the vow she made? Did she worry about whether he'd be cold at night or eat properly or stay healthy?

Scripture doesn't tell us what Hannah felt. It does, however, tell us what she did—she praised God. She acknowledged His holiness and affirmed that He was her rock. She proclaimed His power, sovereignty, justice, and strength. She honored God with her words and modeled total surrender at a time when her heart may have been breaking. In doing so, she performed an act of worship.

Hannah's example inspires us to worship too. How can we do that in our day-to-day lives? Here are a few suggestions: Begin each morning with a grateful heart, saying, "Thanks for making this day, Lord. I will rejoice and be glad in it!" Release and bless your children when God leads them into overseas missionary service or career ministry. Trust Him when He gives you an assignment that's too big for you. Love a spouse who's difficult to live with. Perform mundane chores cheerfully. Visit the elderly or shut-ins. Give God tithes and offerings. The list is endless. Anything you do becomes an act of worship when it brings God pleasure.

God deserves our worship. Romans 12:1 commands us to give it to Him because He's been so merciful to us. Let's follow the example of women like Hannah who worshipped no matter what. And let's remember that worship has nothing to do with how we feel. Worship is based in the character of God, and that never changes.

Inward Glimpse

Heavenly Father, You're worthy of worship no matter what. Teach me to walk in worship day by day. Amen.

- How does Hannah's example inspire you to worship in the midst of your present circumstances?
- Read the hymn "O Worship the King." Which stanza best expresses your heartfelt worship to God?

Outward Glance

Father, satisfy _____ in the morning with Your unfailing love that she might sing for joy and be glad through her whole life (Psalm 90:14). Show her Your deeds and splendor (Psalm 90:16). And as she begins to understand more of who You are, create within her a heart of worship. Amen.

One More Peek

Yet a time is coming and has now come when the true worshippers will worship the Father in spirit and truth, for they are the kind of worshippers the Father seeks. God is spirit, and his worshippers must worship in spirit and in truth (John 4:23-24).

O Worship the King

Robert Grant

O worship the King, all glorious above,
O gratefully sing His power and His love;
Our Shield and Defender, the Ancient of Days,
Pavilioned in splendor, and girded with praise.

O tell of His might, O sing of His grace,
Whose robe is the light, whose canopy space.
His chariots of wrath the deep thunderclouds form,
And dark is His path on the wings of the storm.

Thy bountiful care what tongue can recite?
It breathes in the air, it shines in the light,
It streams from the hills, it descends to the plain,
And sweetly distills in the dew and the rain.

Frail children of dust, and feeble as frail,
In Thee do we trust, nor find Thee to fail:
Thy mercies how tender! how firm to the end!
Our Maker, Defender, Redeemer and Friend.

The Servant

Do good to your servant, and I will live;
I will obey your word.

PSALM 119:17

Upward Gaze

Great and marvelous are Your deeds, Lord God Almighty.
Just and true are Your ways, King of the ages. You alone are
holy. All nations will worship before You, for Your righteous
acts have been revealed (Revelation 15:3-4). Your Word
describes Your character and reveals that You are indeed a
trustworthy and good Master. I'm privileged to serve You.
Amen.

~

Oh, no. Not again! thought Winnie as she entered her living room.
Her houseplants were nowhere to be seen. She looked out the window,
and sure enough, there they were—adorning the front lawn.

Winnie and her husband had recently moved to the Philippines, where she'd hired a woman to help with household chores. For some reason, the servant thought Winnie's houseplants belonged outside, so that's where she placed them every morning. Each evening, Winnie retrieved them and asked her to leave them inside. Playing houseplant tug-o'-war became a daily routine.

One evening, Winnie grew frustrated. "I want the plants to remain in the house," she explained. "This is the way I do it. You might not understand why, but please do what I say." The words had barely left her lips before the Lord's still small voice spoke to her heart.

"Winnie, this has been a visible lesson for you. You don't always understand My ways, but you need to listen to My words and do things My way because you're My servant."

Winnie grimaced. The words rang true. She immediately recalled an incident a week or two prior in which she'd sensed the Lord prompting her to set aside her household tasks and spend time in prayer. *I don't understand why I should stop what I'm doing and pray,* she thought. She chose not to obey the Master's wishes and baked bread instead.

Poor choice. Not only did she miss the blessing that comes from obedience, but the entire bread batch burned.

Scripture is clear: God is the Master, and believers are His servants. And because we're His servants, we're here to do His bidding whether we understand it or not. Sounds so easy, doesn't it? And it should be.

Trouble is, we often hesitate or refuse because we're comfortable doing things our way or we can't visualize the outcome. Sometimes we're afraid of the risk involved. Other times, we can't comprehend His reason for asking us to do something.

Scripture contains numerous accounts that show how God's servants responded to His commands. Take Joshua, for instance. He became the Israelites' leader after Moses died. One day, God appeared to Joshua and issued specific directions to defeat their enemies hiding behind Jericho's walls.

"March around the city once with all the armed men. Do this for six days. Have seven priests carry trumpets of rams' horns in front of the ark. On the seventh day, march around the city seven times with the priests blowing the trumpets. When you hear them sound a long blast on the trumpets, have all the people give a loud shout; then the wall of the city will collapse and the people will go up, every man straight in" (Joshua 6:3-5).

The Master stated His wishes. The servant obeyed. The city was destroyed. Simple.

The outcome might have been a lot different if Joshua had heard the instructions and replied, "I don't understand why You want us to walk around the city once a day for six days. I think twice a day for three days is sufficient. And seven times on the seventh day sounds like overkill. We'll settle for three times on the fourth day. And what's with the trumpets? Sheesh—that's gonna blow our eardrums. Forget the instruments."

Thankfully for the Israelites, Joshua knew and trusted his Master wholeheartedly (Numbers 32:12). When the Israelites approached Jericho, the Lord appeared to him. Joshua fell on his face in reverence and asked, "What message does my Lord have for his servant?" (Joshua 5:14). He heard and obeyed. His relationship with God laid the foundation for his obedience.

The same holds true for us. If we have a personal relationship with Jesus Christ, we are God's servants. He's our Master, and He's a good one. We needn't be afraid or hesitant about obeying His commands. Even if they seem odd or ridiculous, we can trust Him. He knows what He wants done and how He wants to do it. We simply need to listen to His words and do as He says.

Inward Glimpse

Dear Father, thank You for being a good Master. Help me be a worthy, obedient servant. Amen.

- Read the hymn "Take My Life, and Let it Be." How can you serve the Master with your hands? Your feet? Your voice? Your money?

- Write a prayer of consecration, committing yourself fully to serving the Lord.

Outward Glance

Father, according to Your Word, do good to Your servant, _____. Teach her knowledge and good judgment because she believes in Your commands (Psalm 119:65-66). Thank You for delighting in her well-being. Loose her tongue to speak of Your righteousness and of Your praises all day long (Psalm 35:27-28). Amen.

One More Peek

Guard my life, for I am devoted to you.
  You are my God; save your servant
  who trusts in you (Psalm 86:2).

Take My Life, and Let It Be

Frances R. Havergal

Take my life, and let it be
Consecrated, Lord, to Thee;
Take my hands, and let them move
At the impulse of Thy love,
At the impulse of Thy love.

Take my feet, and let them be
Swift and beautiful for Thee;
Take my voice, and let me sing
Always, only, for my King,
Always, only, for my King.

Take my lips, and let them be
Filled with messages for Thee;
Take my silver and my gold,
Not a mite would I withhold,
Not a mite would I withhold.

Take my love, my God, I pour
At Thy feet its treasure store;
Take myself and I will be
Ever, only, all for Thee,
Ever, only, all for Thee.

Housecleaning

Therefore, if anyone is in Christ, he is a new creation;
the old has gone, the new has come!

2 CORINTHIANS 5:17

Upward Gaze

God, I praise You for forgiving all my sins and healing all my diseases. You do not treat me as my sins deserve or repay me according to my iniquities because Your love is as high as the heavens are above the earth toward those who fear You. As far as the east is from the west, so far have You removed my transgressions from me (Psalm 103:3,10-12). Amen.

∽

Two years after we returned from Nepal, Gene and I began searching for a piece of property on which to build a house. We discovered the ideal lot—lakefront, flat yard, sandy beach. There was only one drawback: It held a run-down two-story house inhabited by a human packrat.

The building's condition made the price affordable. We signed the purchase agreement and took possession. Then the work began. For the next 14 months or so, we spent weekends sorting and removing the owner's left-behind belongings.

One room contained an old dresser stuffed with women's blouses, stockings, skirts, and other garments. Apparently, after his wife's death, the man didn't know what to do with her belongings, so he stashed them in the basement.

Another room contained old tires, several televisions, a hot water heater, a toilet, and a radio. Each item either needed fixing or was beyond repair. Cigar boxes, car parts, 30-year-old magazines, light fixtures, and batteries littered the sun porch. Yellowed newspapers hid the floor. Several dozen garbage-filled sacks reeked behind the house.

We bought an old pickup truck and ran like yo-yos to and from the recycle depot and local landfill. The house looked hopeful after we hauled away the last load, but a bad smell permeated the entire structure.

We asked advice from a remodeling professional. "I wouldn't go near that place," he said. He referred us to a demolitionist. That fellow muttered something about asbestos, declined his services, and then suggested the local fire department. "Sometimes they need old structures for practice burns," he said. We followed his counsel, called the chief, and scheduled a date to bring the house down. Neighbors came from far and wide to watch as flames consumed it.

In its place, we built a new two-story house. What a difference! We dedicated it to the Lord and asked Him to make it a place to refresh other people. Before long, we hosted missionary families from countries including the Philippines, Cameroon, Nigeria, Japan, and Nepal. We threw swimming parties for children's Sunday school classes, held year-end ceremonies for our daughters' Girl Guides' club, and hosted barbecues for our son's baseball team. Our home became a tool for blessing many lives. But it wouldn't have been possible without doing some major housecleaning, demolition, and reconstruction first.

In a sense, our lives are like houses. We defile them by storing jealousy or bitterness within our walls. Worry and envy add to the trash buildup. Impure thoughts and self-centeredness contribute to the debris. The filth jeopardizes our spiritual health. It renders us ineffective and robs us of opportunities to bless others.

When we surrender our lives to Christ, He removes the filth. Sometimes, to give us a fresh start, He demolishes old lifestyles and then rebuilds according to His plan and specification. The new always supersedes the old.

God wants our lives to bless others. Through us, He can love our spouses and children. He can refresh weary women concerned about their strained marriage or their kids' choices. He can strengthen a new mom who's lacking sleep. He can encourage our pastors' wives or other ministry leaders.

Let's purpose to live godly lives, keeping ourselves free from sin's trash. And let's be encouraged by knowing that if we sin, Christ will cleanse us.

Inward Glimpse

Dear Father, thank You for Your willingness to cleanse me from all unrighteousness. Please help me live in a way that honors You. Amen.

- Are you storing trash within your walls? If so, what is it? Ask the Lord to remove it so He can bless others through you as fully as He desires.
- Memorize 1 John 1:9 (today's "One More Peek" verse).

Outward Glance

Father, by Your grace, teach _____ to say no to ungod-liness and worldly passions and to live a self-controlled, upright, and godly life. Help her to live in the knowledge that You gave Yourself to redeem her from all wickedness and to purify her so she might be Yours, eager to do what is good (Titus 2:11-14). Amen.

One More Peek

If we confess our sins, he is faithful and just and will forgive us our sins and purify us from all unrighteousness (1 John 1:9).

Honesty and Used Cars

The LORD detests lying lips,
but he delights in men who are truthful.

PROVERBS 12:22

Upward Gaze

Father, because You are the God of truth, I can trust You to teach me Your paths. Guide me in Your truth and teach me, for You are God my Savior, and my hope is in You all day long (Psalm 25:4-5). Amen.

~

After a collision totaled our family's Geo, my husband scoured local auto trader magazines, studied the classified ads, and searched the Internet for a suitable replacement vehicle. We didn't want a fancy car—just something small, in good condition, and economical for our youngest daughter, Kim, to drive to and from school.

When family matters took us to Vancouver, we visited several used car lots in the big city. But each car in our price range had too much rust, too many dings, or way too many miles. Every car, that is, except a little red Geo parked in the far corner of a tiny dealership.

Two salesmen descended within seconds of our setting foot on the lot. "You like this car?" one asked. He popped the hood open. "It's in great shape."

The other fellow slipped into the driver's seat and turned the key in the ignition. Nothing happened. He tried again. We heard a click this time. Gene glanced at me and grinned.

"It's flooded, that's all," said the one with his head under the hood. "I know this car well. It used to be mine. Great car. I took good care of it."

Gene's eyebrows shot up. He flashed another grin. "Thanks, guys, but I think we'll keep looking," he said. "There's no way he's telling the truth," he whispered to me as we walked away.

A week later, Kim and I stopped at a different used car dealership. "I want a hippy van," she'd told her dad and me. "An orange one. You know, the kind with wild flowers painted all over it."

And there it sat. A hippy van. An orange one—minus the wild flowers, but oh well. A woman can't always have *everything* she wants.

Kim climbed into the driver's seat. I climbed in beside her. And before we blinked, the salesman appeared. I braced myself, wondering what to say if he pressured me to buy the van. I needn't have worried.

"Don't vaste your time," he said. "Dis van ees no goot." He chomped into his sandwich. "Da floor—eet has holes. Da sides—der's no steel. Eet's all bondo. Dis van needs a home vit a velder—he can feex eet. Beleef me—you don't vant dis van." He shrugged, smacked the orange scrap-metal-on-wheels, and walked away.

Kim and I waited until he was out of earshot, and then we laughed until we cried. We'd never heard such brutal honesty. The man spoke the truth even though it meant losing a customer, and by doing so, he earned our trust. If he'd had a suitable replacement car for us, we would have happily made a deal with him.

In many cases, our society doesn't place high value on honesty and truthfulness. Rather, it stresses protecting one's personal interests. If lying helps sell a little red car, great! If stretching the truth earns a promotion or gives someone an inflated impression of our abilities, so be it.

God says otherwise. As a man, He declared, "I am the way and the truth and the life" (John 14:6). He personifies truth; therefore He values truth. And we who have a personal relationship with Jesus Christ are His representatives; therefore we are called to live and speak truth.

Honesty in everyday situations, like returning excess change at the grocery store or recording our work hours accurately, may seem trivial. But they're tests that prepare us for bigger opportunities to practice truthfulness. And when we pass those tests, God smiles. He receives honor, and we establish a reputation as being trustworthy women.

PS: Does anyone know what bondo is?

Inward Glimpse

Dear Lord, thank You for being truth. Because Your Holy Spirit lives in me, I can walk in honesty and truthfulness. Amen.

- Do any areas in your life need a truth makeover? If so, what are they? Ask the Lord to forgive you. Thank Him that the Holy Spirit is able to create truth in your innermost being.
- Psalm 51:6 says, "Surely you desire truth in the inner parts; you teach me wisdom in the inmost place." Memorize it. Pray it daily for yourself.

Outward Glance

Father, please teach _____ Your way. Teach her to walk in Your truth. Give her an undivided heart that she may fear Your name (Psalm 86:11). Amen.

One More Peek

For the law was given through Moses; grace and truth came through Jesus Christ (John 1:17).

Just Do It

*I am the Lord's servant...may it
be to me as you have said.*

Luke 1:38

Upward Gaze

Father, I praise You with all my inmost being. My spirit
rejoices in You, my Savior, for You have been mindful of me,
Your servant. You have done great things for me—holy is
Your name (Luke 1:47-49). Amen.

~

One Sunday morning in 2000, Wendy Hagar sat in church and listened to a missionary describe hardships faced by thousands of
orphans and abandoned children in the former Soviet Union. She'd
heard similar stories before, but this time they captured her attention
and moved her with compassion. As she placed a donation in the
offering plate, she sensed the Holy Spirit whisper, *Simply giving money
isn't enough. I'm requiring more of you.*

Wendy recalled her prayer during a 40-day fast one year prior: *God, make me more effective in Your kingdom.* At that time, she'd fully committed herself to obeying whatever He asked. When the service ended, she visited the missionary's display. She saw cloth bags containing handmade overalls and mitts for needy children. In her heart, she knew what God was asking her to do. Before the day ended, Wendy had promised to sew 100 baby overalls, 100 pairs of mitts, and sew and stuff 100 gift bags with 20 items each.

Funny thing was, Wendy hated sewing.

"Are you crazy?" a friend asked. "What are you doing?" her husband and teens asked. "Where will you find time to do this?" Besides being a wife and mother, Wendy worked nearly 40 hours a week for her denomination's women's ministry. But nothing could discourage her.

The next morning Wendy bought more than 175 yards of cloth for the gift bags. A week later she purchased and dyed more than 145 yards of diaper flannel for baby overalls. She visited thrift stores and bought several dozen nearly new baby T-shirts. When other customers asked why she bought so many, she said, "They're going to orphanages!" News of her project spread. So did her enthusiasm.

Within two weeks, mountains of material filled her spare bedroom. Donations such as coloring books, crayons, toothbrushes, pencils, shampoo, soap, and candy poured in. Several individuals gave cash to help cover her expenses. Others volunteered to cut and sew. Wendy purchased hockey duffel bags, stuffed them with the gift bags, and sent them overseas with short-term missionaries. A well-known Christian ministry gave her free storage space in their 5000-square-foot warehouse.

Wendy recently gave me a tour of the warehouse. Cardboard boxes and clear plastic storage containers fill shelf upon shelf. Fabric, backpacks, toiletries, toys, purses, school supplies, clothing—you name it, it's there. But not for long. Her volunteers package and ship those goods before they gather dust.

Wendy's ministry (www.sewonfire.com) has grown to include personalized bags for children, single moms, widows, seniors, and the homeless. So far, they've blessed more than 60,000 people in 55 countries including Tibet, Kosovo, Uganda, Peru, Sudan, India, and

Israel. Is that exciting or what? And all because one woman said yes to God.

Wendy's unconditional obedience reminds me of another woman—Mary, the mother of Jesus. When the angel appeared and told her that she would become pregnant and bear God's Son, she naturally asked a couple questions. I can't say I blame the girl—I might have done the same thing, considering the circumstances. But she didn't argue. ("Do You have any idea what this could do to my reputation? Don't You care about my relationship with Joseph?") She didn't hesitate. ("Now wait a minute. You can't just dump this on me and expect me to agree without thinking about it.") Instead, she readily embraced the plan: "I am the Lord's servant...may it be to me as you have said" (Luke 1:38).

God wants our obedience. He deserves it. But we often hesitate. The thought of trusting an unseen God with an unknown future— our future—seems scary, especially when He asks something that defies human logic. But when we learn to rest in His sovereignty, knowledge, wisdom, power, and love, we find freedom and joy in obedience. That doesn't mean the journey will be trouble free, but like Wendy and Mary, we experience His presence with us and His ability through us.

Inward Glimpse

Dear Father, thank You for being trustworthy. Help me respond to Your commands with an instant "Yes, Lord!" Amen.

- In what specific issues has God asked for your obedience? How have you responded?
- Read Mary's response to God in Luke 1:46-55. List God's character qualities that she mentions. Praise Him that He's still the same today and can equip you to do what He's asking you to do.

Outward Glance

Father, I pray that _____ will serve You with gladness and come before You with joyful songs. May she understand that You made her and that she is Yours. May she enter Your gates with thanksgiving and Your courts with praise. May she understand that You are good, Your love endures forever, and Your faithfulness continues through all generations (Psalm 100). Amen.

One More Peek

His mother said to the servants, "Do whatever he tells you" (John 2:5).

Diamonds and Other Little Treasures

*They will celebrate your abundant goodness
and joyfully sing of your righteousness.*

PSALM 145:7

Upward Gaze

Father, I celebrate Your abundant goodness! Thank You for storing up great goodness for those who fear You and bestowing goodness on those who take refuge in You (Psalm 31:19). I praise Your name!

~

The other day, I heard a wonderful story that illustrates God's goodness in life's little matters. Peggy, her sister, and her mother were enjoying their annual "girls' getaway" at a Florida resort. One afternoon as Peggy fidgeted with her engagement ring, she felt something rough. She glanced at the band and saw that two prongs had snapped off and the ¼-carat diamond was gone. Her heart sank. *Oh no! What am I going to do? How could this have happened? Lord, help me find it!*

Peggy's heart told her not to panic and that the diamond could be replaced. But as she recalled the night she'd received the ring, she couldn't dismiss the sentimental value it held. Throughout the day, she retraced her steps and searched for the stone. She'd shopped at a grocery store, but looking up and down its aisles for the gem yielded nothing. She scoured her car but came up empty-handed. She examined the bathroom floor in her hotel room, checked the carpet around her bed, and hunted through her suitcase. Nothing.

That night Peggy decided to check the hotel's pool deck. She'd taken a morning swim—perhaps it fell out on the deck or in the water itself. Darkness had already fallen, so a hotel employee lent her a flashlight. She and her sister scrutinized the deck like a couple of bloodhounds sniffing for lost treasure.

An elderly gentleman watched their movements awhile and then approached them. "Excuse me—are you looking for something?"

"I am," Peggy said. "I lost the diamond from my ring today. I thought it might be around the pool somewhere."

"I'll get my son," the man said. "He's a professional diver. If your diamond is in the water, and if anyone can find it, he can."

Several minutes later, the man's son appeared and entered the pool. Peggy watched from the deck as he scoured the area near the drain. Sure enough, when he broke the water's surface, he held the diamond between his thumb and index finger!

Sometimes God's goodness leaves us breathless, especially when it involves His attention to the little desires of our heart. After all, in the vast scheme of life and eternity, how important is a replaceable diamond? Yet He heard Peggy's prayer and responded because He knew it mattered to His daughter.

I've heard similar stories that show God's goodness. For instance, a less fortunate family couldn't afford Christmas gifts. The parents felt heartbroken because they couldn't buy their young daughter the doll she'd hoped for. On Christmas Eve, a boxful of gifts was delivered to their door. It contained—you guessed it—the exact doll she'd wanted.

For a couple of years after my Bible college graduation, I worked as a dean of high school girls. I enjoyed inviting the students to my home for dinner and often wished I had a nice salad bowl set—a wooden one, to be exact. My meager salary made it impossible to buy extras, so I began asking God to provide. Within a few weeks, a friend said, "I have a wooden salad bowl set I never use. Would you like it?"

What motivates God to pay attention to and grant us our heart's trivial desires? It's not because He doesn't have anything else to do. After all, He keeps track of nearly 6,400,000,000 men, women, and children. He governs national and international politics. He holds the sun, moon, and stars in place. He sets the sea's boundary and controls the earth's temperature and seasonal changes. He listens for a sinner's cry, comforts the mourning, and heals the sick. How's that for basics?

Perhaps God responds to His children this way because He embodies goodness. And maybe He revels in our joy-filled response at His surprises.

Thankfully, in His wisdom, He doesn't give us everything we want. And because His goal is to make us Christlike (rather than merely happy), He knows when to answer our prayers with a yes and when He should refuse or wait. Either way, His goodness never fails those who are living in right relationship with Him.

Inward Glimpse

Dear Father, thank You for caring about those little things that matter to me. Help me reflect the same attitude toward others. Amen.

- Read the hymn "When All Thy Mercies, O My God." As you survey your life, what mercies do you see?
- Write a short prayer thanking God for His goodness toward you.

Outward Glance

Father, I pray that Your goodness and love will follow _____ all the days of her life. Bring her to Your dwelling place forever, for spending eternity with You would be the ultimate good gift (Psalm 23:6). Amen.

One More Peek

"Why do you call me good?" Jesus answered. "No one is good—except God alone" (Mark 10:18).

When All Thy Mercies, O My God

Joseph Addison

When all thy mercies, O my God,
My rising soul surveys,
Transported with the view, I'm lost
In wonder, love, and praise.

Unnumbered comforts to my soul
Thy tender care bestowed,
Before my infant heart conceived
From whom those comforts flowed.

When worn with sickness, oft hast Thou
With health renewed my face;
And, when in sins and sorrows bowed,
Revived my soul with grace.

Through every period of my life
Thy goodness I'll pursue,
And after death, in distant worlds,
The glorious theme renew.

Qualified for the Task

O great and powerful God, whose name is the LORD Almighty,
great are your purposes and mighty are your deeds.

JEREMIAH 32:18-19

Upward Gaze

O, Lord, You appoint the sun to shine by day. You tell the
moon and stars to shine by night. You stir up the sea so its
waves roar—the Lord Almighty is Your name! (Jeremiah
31:35). You alone are God, and into Your hands I place my
life. Amen.

~

We hear women talk about bad hair days. Let me tell ya, I've had a
few. In fact, I've had *horrific* hair days. And all because I trusted
someone who wasn't qualified to cut my locks.

Living in the Himalayas for three years limited my access to experienced hairdressers. About 18 months after moving to our village, I
desperately needed a decent cut. My bangs hung below my chin and
the rest resembled a below-shoulder-length mop.

The layered look would be nice, I thought.

I naively asked a woman from a neighboring village if she could cut hair. "Sure!" she replied. "I cut my sons' hair all the time." That should have been sufficient warning, but somehow, I missed it.

The woman threw a towel across my shoulders and snipped. In a single stroke, she sheared about four inches and took my hairdo to a new level—the nape of my neck. She chopped and snipped and hummed. I sat in stunned silence.

Words can't describe my husband's facial expression when he arrived 20 minutes later. "Well, what do you think?" the hairdresser wannabe asked him.

Gene studied my new "do" from every angle. He cleared his throat. "It's...um...it's...a haircut, that's for sure."

I cried all the way home. "I can't be seen in public," I sputtered. "Please help me." I handed Gene a pair of scissors. "Layer what's left," I begged.

His eyes registered fear. "I've never cut anyone's hair."

"Don't worry, I'll talk you through it." What was I thinking? My plan failed. I cried again, and this time, my poor husband joined me.

Eight months passed before a professional could properly shape my "do." Believe me, as long as I live, I will never rely on a hairdresser wannabe again. Having a trained stylist matters a lot to me! But something else matters far more—knowing that the God who holds my life in His hands is qualified for the task. Scripture explains His credentials.

First, God possesses limitless ability. He poured the sea and scheduled the tides. He sculpted the mountains. He gave sight to the blind, healed the lame, raised the dead. He fed more than 5000 people with five small loaves and two fish. His strength is the same today. He can do anything, and that includes supplying our needs, whatever they are.

God also possesses boundless wisdom: "Oh, the depth of the riches of the wisdom and knowledge of God! How unsearchable his judgments, and his path beyond tracing out!" (Romans 11:33). His wisdom far outweighs ours. He knows everything about everything. Nothing puzzles Him. Better than anything or anyone else, He knows how we should live.

And God possesses endless love. He proved it through Jesus Christ's sacrificial death. Because He loves us that much, He does whatever's necessary to maintain our spiritual well-being. That doesn't mean He gives us everything we want—His goal is not to make us happy but to make us Christlike. In the process, everything He does or allows in our lives is filtered through His heart of love.

God holds our lives in His hands. Is He qualified? Absolutely. Can we trust Him to do the job with excellence? Absolutely. And He'll never disappoint.

Inward Glimpse

Dear Father, thank You for fulfilling Your responsibility with excellence. Help me trust You unceasingly. Amen.

- Describe how God has shown His love toward you in practical ways.
- List three other credentials that prove God's ability to care for you.

Outward Glance

Heavenly Father, help _____ remember that You made her. When she feels afraid or anxious, remind her that You formed her in the womb and You will help her (Isaiah 44:2). Assure her that You alone are God, there is no other like You (Isaiah 46:9), and You alone are qualified to hold her life in Your hands. Amen.

One More Peek

"Though the mountains be shaken
  and the hills be removed,
yet my unfailing love for you will not be shaken
  nor my covenant of peace be removed,"
  says the LORD, who has compassion on you
  (Isaiah 54:10).

Fear of Man

Fear of man will prove to be a snare,
but whoever trusts in the LORD is kept safe.

PROVERBS 29:25

Upward Gaze

God, I praise You for being my light and salvation. You are the stronghold of my life. I needn't be afraid of anyone (Psalm 27:1). Amen.

≈

Martha eyed the phone as she nursed her newborn son. *It's now or never,* she thought. *I can't stall any longer.*

Three months earlier, Martha had taken maternity leave after her first child's birth. She never intended to return—as a first-time mom at age 40, she wanted to savor every minute with her child—but she didn't tell anyone in her office. She feared her coworkers' and manager's response. After all, she was the top salesperson. If she quit, the company would likely suffer financial loss. But another fear troubled her.

They know I'm earning $100,000 a year, she thought. *They'll think I'm nuts if I quit my job to stay home. Besides, the other women in the office juggle parenting and work. They might think I can't handle the challenge or I'm putting my brain on a permanent vacation.*

Martha laid her son in his crib and made the dreaded phone call. To her relief, the branch manager's voice mail answered. *Whew!* thought Martha. *This makes it easy!* She left a message saying that she wouldn't be returning. She justified her decision with a detailed explanation about the baby's time-consuming physical needs. Born a month early, he vomited frequently and suffered breathing problems that required special treatments every two hours. She ended her call. *Done. Hopefully the boss will understand. After all, everything I said is true.*

Martha retrieved her belongings from the office several weeks later. Her coworkers admired the baby and then began asking questions. "You earn so much money—why don't you hire a nanny?" said one.

Martha cringed. She feared their response, but she knew she had to be honest. She drew a deep breath. Heart pounding, she said, "I see the burden that working moms carry, trying to balance their jobs with parenting and maintaining a household. I don't want that stress. Besides, I want to raise my son. I want to see him take his first step. I want to hear his first word. I want to be the one instilling my values into his life." Several women nodded in agreement. Others just stared.

Martha left the office that day feeling relieved. She knew she'd overcome a huge hurdle in her life—the fear of other people. She regretted not being forthright earlier and made a deliberate choice to be honest about her reason for staying home regardless of what others might think of her. That decision led her to discover other moms who felt like she did, and it birthed an exciting ministry that encourages women who share her passion.

Today, Martha's website, www.Christian-Homemaking.com, receives over 12,000 visitors each month. She publishes an e-zine entitled *Wives of Excellence* that ministers to more than 4500 women. Nearly 500 women participate in her online discussion group. They share practical ideas and insights that strengthen their families, and they encourage each other in their faith. Just think! This might not have happened if Martha had continued to let the fear of other people wrap its tendrils around her.

It's easy for us to succumb to such fear. Like Martha, we're often afraid of other people's opinions of us. Perhaps, while volunteering on a decision-making committee, we foresee potential problems with a proposal. But we don't express our concerns because we're afraid everyone will think we're negative.

A conversation with girlfriends turns to gossip. We know it's wrong but zip our lips because we don't want them to think we consider ourselves "super spiritual."

The Lord prompts us to confront a friend involved in an adulterous affair. We refuse. After all, she might dump us for judging her.

Fear will swallow us if we let it. But we can overcome! When we heed God's commands to "fear not" and remember His promised presence with us, we can say and do what is right regardless of what other people think. Granted, we must speak and act in a loving manner. We don't want to be arrogant and earn their disrespect.

God's opinion of us is more important than what others think. When we keep that in perspective, we can find the strength to live beyond the fear of other people's opinions.

Inward Glimpse

Dear Father, thank You for giving me the victory over the fear of what others think. Help me walk in freedom, seeking to please only You in all I do and say. Amen.

- Is the fear of man an issue in your life? If so, what are you afraid of? What can you do about it? What do you want God to do about it? Ask Him to do that.
- Memorize today's key verse—Proverbs 29:25.

Outward Glance

Father, I pray that _____ will trust in You when she is afraid. Teach her to praise Your Word and walk in confidence, knowing that mortal man can't do anything to her (Psalm 56:3-4). Amen.

One More Peek

Am I now trying to win the approval of men, or of God? Or am I trying to please men? If I were still trying to please men, I would not be a servant of Christ (Galatians 1:10).

Peace in the Storm

You will keep in perfect peace
him whose mind is steadfast,
because he trusts in you.

ISAIAH 26:3

Upward Gaze

Father, thank You for giving strength to Your people and blessing them with peace (Psalm 29:11). I rejoice in You because You are near. Your peace transcends all understanding and guards my heart and my mind in Christ Jesus (Philippians 4:4-5,7). Amen.

~

At age 37, Jan heard the words no woman wants to hear: "I must be honest. This does *not* look good. I'd like to do a lumpectomy tomorrow." The petite brunette gave her consent. She left the surgeon's office alone and frightened.

Jan drove to the airport where she waited for her husband to return from an out-of-town business meeting. While waiting, she recalled an evening two months prior. Her husband—a medical doctor—had been at work that night. As her sons, ages five and two, slept, she'd exercised and watched a television documentary about breast cancer. For no known reason, grief welled within her. Sorrow turned to tears, and tears gave way to sobs. *Why is the program affecting me like this?* she'd wondered.

Recalling that night, Jan understood. Through the documentary, the Lord had foreshadowed her future and prepared her for the road ahead. Now it made sense.

The next morning's procedure confirmed malignant cancer. Later, further medical tests questioned whether the lumpectomy had indeed removed all cancer cells. The surgeon recommended a mastectomy and scheduled a date two weeks away.

Once again grief welled within her, but in the midst, Jan experienced deep peace. Bible reading and prayer countered fear and redirected her focus to the Lord. Books by well-known Christian authors encouraged her faith.

Journaling helped process thoughts and emotions. *What's the meaning in all this, God?* she wrote. *Only You know. Our part is to trust You. You have allowed this hurt to happen, but You've brought peace in the midst of the storm. You've given an absolute assurance that You are in control and You will work all things for our good because You love us so very much.*

Trusting in God's never-ending love brought hope when Jan mourned the loss of her breast and felt less feminine. Acknowledging His strength gave courage when weakness overwhelmed her. Recognizing His sovereignty helped her practice thanksgiving and move forward with her life. When a pastor's wife invited her to address a women's group two months post surgery, Jan agreed. She wanted others to know how God had granted peace in the midst of her storm.

What is peace? Some folks think it's the absence of adversity in our lives. If that's the case, peace is unattainable because we'll experience adversity in one way or another until the day we reach heaven. Friction in personal relationships, terrorist threats, job layoffs, financial strain, accidents, illness, war—these problems are here to stay.

True peace is rest in the midst of adversity or storms. How can we attain that? Through understanding the character of God and how it relates to everyday life. For instance, understanding God's ability to provide for our needs enables us to rest despite job cutbacks. Understanding His unconditional love grants peace even when a family member or coworker sends constant criticism our way. And understanding His sovereignty over the future gives peace despite ongoing terrorist threats. When we, like Jan, focus our minds on Him rather than the swirling storms, we know peace.

And we can help others experience peace when they face storms. How? By praying for them—and telling them that we're doing so. Our prayers can make a difference for those who are anxious or hurting.

Regardless of the storms we face, we can experience and model peace by remembering who's in control and the scriptural truths about His character.

Inward Glimpse

Dear Father, thank You for being the source of peace. Keep my mind focused on You rather than the storms. Amen.

- How has God brought peace in the midst of a storm in your life?
- Name someone who is facing a personal storm. Ask the Lord to bring that person to your mind throughout the day, and pray for her when He does. Tell that person that you're praying.

Outward Glance

Dear Lord, please bless _____ and keep her. Make Your face shine upon her and be gracious to her. Turn Your face toward her and give her peace (Numbers 6:24-26). Amen.

One More Peek

The disciples went and woke him, saying, "Master, Master, we're going to drown!" He got up and rebuked the wind and the raging waters; the storm subsided, and all was calm (Luke 8:24).

The Coach

Similarly, if anyone competes as an athlete, he does not receive the victor's crown unless he competes according to the rules.

2 TIMOTHY 2:5

Upward Gaze

Heavenly Father, I praise You for being the strength of my heart and my portion forever (Psalm 73:26). You delight in the way of the man whose steps You have made firm. Though he stumbles, he will not fall, for You uphold him with Your hand (Psalm 37:23-24). Amen.

≈

Ninth-grader Kim joined her school's track and field club, practicing after school several days a week. When summer vacation arrived, her track coach, Kathy, gave her an individualized training schedule.

On several occasions during the summer, Kathy ran with Kim. Drawing from her own successful athletic experience, she shared practical tips such as the importance of pacing oneself and not eating within two hours of a race. She taught Kim several warm-up exercises and invited her to participate in various community races. She encouraged her to finish each race even though she might not win.

Kim responded to Kathy's enthusiasm by following her example and verbal instruction. As a result, her body grew strong and healthy. She discovered an ability she hadn't known existed, and she won several first-place ribbons for her age category. She developed a disciplined pattern of physical exercise and displayed increased self-confidence.

Kim's first six-mile cross-country race led along a forest path, across steep rock faces, and over fallen logs. Even though she didn't know other competitors, she eagerly made her way to the starting line. At the official's signal, she dashed into the woods with more than 70 strangers, mostly adults twice her age. I watched, amazed, remembering the days when she was too shy to answer the phone.

Kathy's coaching spurred tremendous personal growth in my daughter's life. And because Kim realized that her teacher knew what she talked about, Kim followed her advice.

We experience personal growth and success along our life's race when we heed God's advice. As our coach, God wants us to run life's race successfully. Therefore, He teaches us to focus on what's good and right. He commands us to love Him more than anything or anyone else, live as peacemakers, help the poor, speak healing words, confess our sins, and give thanks in everything. He instructs us to shed anything that weighs us down—envy, pride, jealousy, discontentment, gossip, sexual immorality.

Just as Kathy instructed Kim to persevere, God counsels us to never give up. "I press on toward the goal to win the prize for which God has called me heavenward in Christ Jesus," Paul says in Philippians 3:1. God wants us never to give up, even when the race wearies us. Even though we stumble and fall. Even when we want to throw our hands up in the air and cry in defeat, "Enough! I can't go on!"

God understands our feelings when we're weary or afraid of losing our way. He gives us strength and courage to finish the race. Sometimes He offers a much-needed boost through a Scripture promise or a song. At other times, He cheers us along through a friend's prayers, a timely word, or even a good night's sleep. Our divine coach knows what we need when we need it, and He's dedicated to our success. Our task is to follow His counsel and run with endurance the race that is set before us.

Inward Glimpse

Dear Father, thank You for being my coach through life. Help me follow Your counsel and persevere. Amen.

- Are unnecessary weights hindering your progress? If so, what are they?
- Write a prayer asking God to remove those weights.

Outward Glance

Father, I pray that _____ will throw off everything that hinders her and the sin that so easily entangles. Let her run with perseverance the race that is marked for her. Help her fix her eyes on Jesus and, considering His example of perseverance, not grow weary and lose heart (Hebrews 12:1-3). Amen.

One More Peek

He gives strength to the weary
and increases the power of the weak.
Even youths grow tired and weary,
and young men stumble and fall;
but those who hope in the LORD
will renew their strength.
They will soar on wings like eagles;
they will run and not grow weary,
they will walk and not be faint (Isaiah 40:29-31).

Never Alone

Where can I go from your Spirit?
Where can I flee from your presence?
If I go up to the heavens, you are there;
if I make my bed in the depths, you are there.

PSALM 139:7-8

Upward Gaze

I praise You for being omnipresent. You are everywhere—if I go to the heavens, You are there. If I make my bed in the depths, You are there. If I rise on the wings of the dawn or settle on the far side of the sea, even there Your hand will hold me (Psalm 139:6-10). Such knowledge is hard for me to understand, but it's true! Amen.

~

Sally watched from across the delivery room as her 26-year-old daughter, Stacy, rested between contractions. It wouldn't be long now. Sally had anticipated her first grandchild's birth since the moment her daughter shared the good news. But she never dreamed it would be like this. She recalled the nurse's words: "I'm so sorry. There's no heartbeat." *Why, God? Why have You allowed this baby to be stillborn?*

The room emptied as labor dragged on. Sally's son-in-law stepped outside. Her husband, a pastor, retreated to the privacy of another room where he vented his anguish. Her two grown sons stayed behind to hold their sister's hands as contractions peaked. Sally remained too. Her heart wrenched for Stacy. She wanted to rescue her daughter, but there was *absolutely nothing* she could do.

Slowly, slowly, Sally descended into a spiritual pit. Her thoughts played a one-sided conversation: *God, we've had talks about tough times. I told You that I never wanted to experience anything really difficult because I wouldn't be able to be the person You need me to be for our congregation. Remember those talks, God? I don't think a hard time would be good for me...I'd just be a mess.*

Her descent continued. Down, down, down, into a black hole. *I'm going away from You for a while, God,* she said. *When I'm ready, I'll climb out of this hole and come back to You. Then we'll talk again.*

Almost immediately, Sally sensed God's voice. *You're not alone,* He whispered. *I know all about this hole, and I'm here with you. I don't like what's happened any more than you do—it's a result of man's choice when I made him. But Sally, I sent My Son, and He died for you. And because of what He's done, I'm here with you and you have hope.*

His words stopped Sally's descent. Her pain continued; her tears flowed. But her perspective changed as she realized in a fresh way that God was indeed with her, even in her deepest pain.

When Sally told me her story, she said, "Encountering God in that dark, dark pit showed me that no matter where I go, I can't hide from Him. He can be, and He will be, wherever I am, even when I think I'm running away from Him. He's *always* with me, and as a result, I know I can absolutely trust Him whatever comes my way."

Sally compares her experience to Jonah's. He too disliked his circumstances. He too tried to escape God's presence. And he too descended—down, down, down—into a pit. The pit of a fish's stomach. Yuck. Not a pleasant place to be.

But even in the fish's belly, Jonah wasn't alone. God was with him and rushed to his rescue when he cried for help. "To the roots of the mountains I sank down," said Jonah. "The earth beneath barred me in forever. But you brought my life up from the pit, O Lord my God" (Jonah 2:6).

It's easy to feel God's presence when our lives look pretty. We can greet the morning with a smile. We can enjoy reading the Scriptures and talking with the Lord. We can be nice to our kids and our spouse and even smile at strangers in the grocery store.

But when life turns ugly, it can be another story. We can be overwhelmed by the circumstances. We can lose sight of God's presence. We can even feel angry at Him and try to run away. But it's no use. He promised never to leave us, and He doesn't lie.

When we encounter trials, we can pour out our hearts to God because He understands our pain. And we can be encouraged in knowing that because of Christ's death and resurrection, God is with us. We have a Savior who is trustworthy. We have hope.

Inward Glimpse

Dear Father, thank You for Your presence with me at all times. Help me live life with that truth in mind. Amen.

- Augustine said, "In my deepest wound I saw Your glory, and it dazzled me." Has God ever dazzled you with His glory in a dark place? If so, what did you learn about Him?
- Read the hymn "The King of Love My Shepherd Is." What stanza means the most to you and why?

Outward Glance

Father, I pray that _____ will live her life with the knowledge that Your presence surrounds her. When she encounters difficult times, may she recall Your promise to go with her, to never leave or forsake her. And may she find courage and strength in that certainty (Deuteronomy 31:6). Amen.

One More Peek

You hem me in—behind and before;
   you have laid your hand upon me.
Such knowledge is too wonderful for me,
   too lofty for me to attain (Psalm 139:5-6).

The King of Love My Shepherd Is

Henry W. Baker

The King of love my Shepherd is,
Whose goodness faileth never;
I nothing lack if I am His
And He is mine forever.

Where streams of living water flow
My ransomed soul He leadeth,
And, where the verdant pastures grow,
With food celestial feedeth.

Perverse and foolish oft I strayed,
But yet in love He sought me.
And on His shoulder gently laid,
And home rejoicing brought me.

In death's dark vale I fear no ill
With Thee, dear Lord, beside me;
Thy rod and staff my comfort still,
Thy cross before to guide me.

And so through all the length of days
Thy goodness faileth never;
Good Shepherd, may I sing Thy praise
Within Thy house forever.

Whose Understanding?

*Trust in the LORD with all your heart
and lean not on your own understanding.*

PROVERBS 3:5

Upward Gaze

Father, the depth of the riches of Your wisdom and knowledge cannot be measured! Your judgments are unsearchable and your paths beyond tracing out (Romans 11:33). The immensity of Your understanding causes me to stand in awe of who You are. Amen.

~

Betty shoved an electric frying pan into the kitchen cupboard and slammed the door. "This stupid kitchen is impossible to work in. I can't even turn around in it. And look at that pantry—it will never hold all our stuff!" She stormed from the kitchen, ran to the master bedroom, and threw herself across the bed. Tears streamed down her face. *This is impossible,* she thought. *I can't live here!*

Several weeks earlier, her husband, David, landed a great job in a city several hours' drive from where they'd lived for years. They sold their family home and spent three weekends scouring for a suitable house in what they considered the ideal neighborhood, but they found nothing.

Feeling pressed for time, the couple bought a house in a different neighborhood. Their 3000-square-foot purchase met almost every requirement on their "must have" list, plus a few extras—hot tub, private landscaped backyard, plenty of space for hosting overnight guests, and an enormous deck. It's only drawback? The location was dry and unappealing, not fertile and lush like their previous region or the area in which they'd hoped to live.

For six months Betty struggled to accept their location. She felt displaced. She desperately missed the green lawns and gardens she'd enjoyed her entire life. Even though she and David had agreed together to purchase this home, she partially blamed him for her unhappiness: *You dragged our family out here. You made me live in this house.*

All the while, Betty knew she was throwing a pity party. She felt like a little girl stomping her foot and saying, "I don't want to feel better." She knew where she longed to live, and she didn't want the answer to be no.

But God's answer was no. And for a very good reason.

Nine months after Betty's family moved, one of the worst forest fires in British Columbia's history blazed through her city. The fire razed more than 200 expensive houses in a single night, destroying the neighborhood in which she'd so desperately wanted to live. The flames left families destitute. Landscaped yards resembled a moonscape. But Betty and her family were spared because they lived in a different vicinity— the one she'd originally resented. Through a rare and graphic demonstration, Betty realized how God had protected her from her own wants.

When Betty told me her story, I immediately thought of today's verse. It's a wonderful reminder for us, isn't it? But sometimes it sounds so trite. So "Christianese." Easy to agree with when life hands us everything we want. Not so easy to swallow when we don't get our way or can't understand why things happen as they do. But that's exactly when we need to cling to its truth.

When we encounter situations we don't understand or appreciate, we *can* trust in the Lord. Why? Because He knows the future. We don't.

And since He knows what lies ahead, He knows what's best for us. (Hmm...there's that Christian lingo again.) The fact is, God's understanding is bigger than ours. Period. And that's why we can trust Him with all our heart.

The truth of today's key verse can encourage us when we face situations we don't understand. Rather than wasting our energy worrying, manipulating, or trying to figure things out, we can place our trust in the Lord and know that He has everything in control. He will see us through.

Inward Glimpse

Dear Father, thank You for being trustworthy. Please move that truth beyond my head and into the deepest recesses of my heart. Amen.

- Have you experienced a situation that caused you to apply the truth of Proverbs 3:5? How did you gain a better understanding of God's character through it?
- Name a situation that's requiring you to trust the Lord with all your heart. Write a short prayer committing it to Him. Ask Him to help you refrain from leaning on your own understanding.

Outward Glance

Dear Father, please help _____ trust in You rather than in her own understanding. When she lacks contentment or feels worried or frightened, remind her that You have stored up great goodness for those who fear You, and give her peace (Psalm 31:19). Amen.

One More Peek

For the LORD gives wisdom,
 and from his mouth come knowledge and understanding
 (Proverbs 2:6).

God Speaks

My sheep listen to my voice;
I know them, and they follow me.

JOHN 10:27

Upward Gaze

Father, may all the kings of the earth praise You when they hear Your words. May they sing of Your ways, for Your glory is great (Psalm 138:4-5). Amen.

~

A month before Christmas, Elizabeth received a nice-sized check for work she'd done. As she pondered what to do with the money, she thought about a fellow she'd met at a Christian conference. She knew his family struggled financially. *I wonder how their situation affects his wife,* she thought.

Elizabeth understood financial hardship. She knew the frustration of shopping for clothes on the reject rack or of settling for cheap but unsatisfactory haircuts. Feeling compelled to bless the woman, she wrote a note: "I don't know you. I don't know what you need. But this is for you, not for your kids' Christmas gifts. Buy yourself something that's not on sale and treat yourself to a good haircut." She enclosed a $200 check and mailed the letter.

The woman's response arrived a week later. Elizabeth could hardly contain her joy when she read the note: "How did you know? I'm pregnant and I feel so dowdy. I've been longing for a decent haircut—I even asked the Lord to provide one. But I've felt so worried about buying the kids' Christmas presents that I haven't spent any money on myself. Through your gift, God said yes to the haircut. If He can take care of that, I have no doubt He'll look after my children as well."

I love hearing stories like this! They prove that God speaks to His children. How does He do that? Author Kilian Haley wrote that He "comes right into our mind. Our thoughts are not only our thoughts; our desires are not only our desires—they may also be God's thoughts and desires.... He speaks secretly, noiselessly, as befits the Divinity."[3]

Elizabeth's thoughts weren't her own. She could not possibly have known the woman's desire for a decent haircut. Only God knew, and He communicated that knowledge to her.

Our family experienced a similar incident. As missionaries, we rely on the financial support of friends and family. A year after entering this ministry, a national postal strike prevented some checks from reaching us. I first looked at our dwindling bank account and then peeked into our cupboards and fridge, and I wondered how I would buy groceries if the strike continued. No one knew of our dilemma—except God.

Several weeks prior, we'd invited friends to our home for dinner on a particular day. That day arrived, and I scraped a few fixins' together for a casserole but wondered how I'd feed my family afterward. Imagine my shock and delight when our guests arrived with six or seven sacks filled with groceries!

"Why did you do this?" I asked.

I'll never forget the husband's reply: "We just felt we should."

Our friends' thoughts were not their own. They'd not made the connection between the postal strike and our practical needs. Their thoughts were clearly God's thoughts, communicated secretly and noiselessly.

Some folks think God speaks only to the so-called super-spiritual. Not so. He speaks to anyone who walks in right relationship with Him. When our hearts are ready not only to hear but also to obey, as

Elizabeth and our friends did, we can expect to hear Him. Tricia McCary Rhodes says this:

> When we walk with God, taking the time to set our hearts aright before Him, we can be confident that He will speak. As we still and quiet our souls, expecting Him to reveal Himself, He responds. And when He does, we know we have heard Him.[4]

Take the time to set your heart right before Him. Be still. Expect Him to speak. And keep your spiritual ears open. May you enjoy an ever-increasing sensitivity to God's secret, noiseless voice!

Inward Glimpse

Dear Father, thank You for wanting to speak to me. Help me hear Your voice and obey Your words. Amen.

- Describe a situation in which you heard God speak. How did you respond? What happened?
- What might hinder you from hearing God speak?

Outward Glance

Father, I pray that _____ will live with a noble and pure heart. May she hear Your Word and retain it and, by persevering, produce a crop (Luke 8:15). And when she seeks direction, may she hear Your voice behind her, saying, "This is the way; walk in it" (Isaiah 30:21). Amen.

One More Peek

Blessed is the man who listens to me,
*   watching daily at my doors,*
*   waiting at my doorway.*
For whoever finds me finds life
*   and receives favor from the LORD* (Proverbs 8:34-35).

Forgiveness

If you, O LORD, kept a record of sins,
O Lord, who could stand?
But with you there is forgiveness;
therefore you are feared.

PSALM 130:3-4

Upward Gaze

Heavenly Father, I praise You because You are kind and forgiving. You abound in love to all who call to You (Psalm 86:5). Even though I don't deserve Your forgiveness, You give it because of Your character—gracious, compassionate, and slow to anger (Nehemiah 9:17). Thank You! Amen.

∽

Elaine sat across the kitchen table from her husband and stared in disbelief. "You've never loved me?" she asked in a whisper.

"Never," he said. "And now I want out."

Elaine reeled. Their two-year union had been difficult, but she'd always thought their relationship would survive despite the struggles. Her husband's confession shattered that assumption. He'd met a former girlfriend at a high school reunion and had an affair. He planned to divorce Elaine and marry the other woman.

Thankfully, his plans never materialized. Twenty-seven years later, Elaine and her husband are still married. She credits forgiveness, extended by each to the other, as the glue that's held their marriage together through various emotional cracks and chips.

But she's quick to admit that their ability to forgive each other's shortcomings hasn't come from within themselves. Rather, it's come from understanding that because God has forgiven their own sins, they can, and must, by His grace, forgive each other.

The same understanding holds true for us in situations we face. Say, for instance, a coworker spreads a nasty rumor about us. Perhaps she's insecure. Maybe she's jealous. Regardless of her motives, her actions are wrong. How should we respond?

The natural tendency might be to retaliate with a juicy tidbit of our own. Or we could shun her. We're justified, aren't we? Or…we could forgive. Is it easy? No, but it's necessary. If we have a personal relationship with Jesus Christ, He's forgiven us and expects us to extend the same grace to others.

"To be a Christian means to forgive the inexcusable, because God has forgiven the inexcusable in you," said C.S. Lewis. Such wise words! When we've been hurt or offended by someone, we're often tempted to nurse the wound or bear the grudge. We're prone to lash out in self-defense, to protect our pride and our reputation. However, if we heed Lewis' advice, we refuse to follow our natural inclinations and follow the Lord's example instead.

What does true forgiveness look like? In his book *The Freedom of Forgiveness*, David Augsburger writes,

> Forgiving is self-giving with no self-seeking. It gives love where the enemy expects hatred. It gives freedom where the enemy deserves punishment. It gives understanding where the enemy anticipates anger and revenge. Forgiveness refuses to seek its

own advantage. It gives back to the other person his freedom and his future.[5]

That's exactly what Jesus Christ did for us! He endured whippings and beatings. He withstood people spitting in His face and mocking His authority. He could have commanded lightning bolts to strike dead His false accusers and the guards who mocked Him. Instead, He gave His life without reserve when He took the punishment for our sins. He prayed, "Father, forgive them. They don't know what they're doing." And by doing so, He restored freedom and a future to those who place their saving faith in Him.

When we think about what Jesus Christ did for us, how can we even consider withholding forgiveness from one who offends us? Extending forgiveness is never easy, but it's not optional in God's eyes. Withholding forgiveness places chains around our heart. It breeds bitterness. It builds a wall between us and the offender—and worse, between us and God.

But following His example sets us free. It breaks the chains, banishes bitterness, razes the walls, and rebuilds broken relationships. Elaine's marriage proves it. When we've been hurt, let's remember to follow Christ's example and choose forgiveness.

Inward Glimpse

Dear Father, thank You for giving Your life so that I might know forgiveness for my sin. Help me follow Your example and forgive those who hurt me. Amen.

- Are you withholding forgiveness in any area of your life? What will you benefit by doing so? What steps can you take to practice forgiveness in this situation?

- On a piece of scrap paper, list at least five sins for which God has forgiven you. Now rip up the paper and throw it away. Write a prayer thanking God for the freedom of forgiveness.

Outward Glance

Lord, I pray that _____ will be kind and compassionate to others. When others offend her, may she remember what You've done for her and, in turn, extend forgiveness to them (Ephesians 4:32). Amen.

One More Peek

For he has rescued us from the dominion of darkness and brought us into the kingdom of the Son he loves, in whom we have redemption, the forgiveness of sins (Colossians 1:13-14).

The Silver Tray

The ransomed of the LORD will return.
They will enter Zion with singing;
everlasting joy will crown their heads.
Gladness and joy will overtake them,
and sorrow and sighing will flee away.

ISAIAH 51:11

Upward Gaze

Heavenly Father, You appoint the sun to shine by day and the moon and stars to shine by night. You stir up the sea so that its waves roar (Jeremiah 31:35). In Your power You rule the universe, but in Your mercy You stoop to shield the one who wanders in a barren land (Deuteronomy 32:10-13). Thank You for restoring what the locusts have eaten and working wonders to replace one's shame. I praise Your name (Joel 2:25-27). Amen.

∾

Two sisters, ages five and eight, were pedaling their bikes toward home when a garbage truck rumbled past. As it slowed to turn a corner, a shiny metal object rolled from the vehicle's open back and clattered on the road.

"What's that?" the younger girl asked. "Let's go see!" She pedaled her bicycle faster.

"Leave it!" said the older sister. "It's dirty."

The five-year-old ignored the command. She jumped off her bike and retrieved the object. "Look—it's a tray." She wiped it with her hand. "Let's take it home."

"What for?" asked the other girl. "No one can use it. It's garbage. Throw it away!"

Again the younger sister refused to listen. She tucked the tray under her arm and walked her bike home. Minutes later she showed the treasure to her mother.

"It's just tarnished," said her mom. "Let's wash and polish it. It might be very pretty when it's clean." She was right. A delicate etched floral pattern adorned the tray's silver face. Rather than being tossed out as trash, it soon served a useful purpose in their home.

That tray, stashed in my cupboard today, depicts many women's lives. As a retreat speaker, I hear countless stories from women who grew up in abusive situations and left home feeling tarnished. Some have endured endless criticism and consider themselves worthless. Some tell me they've struggled with alcohol or drug addiction. Others bear emotional scars after choosing an abortion or having an affair. Satan loves to discourage these gals. "You're dirty," he taunts. "Trash. Worthless."

Stormie is one of the most moving autobiographies I've read. In its pages, bestselling author Stormie Omartian tells of her traumatic childhood, which eventually led her to drugs, the occult, devastating relationships, and an unsuccessful suicide attempt. Her life continued its downward spiral until a pastor introduced her to Jesus Christ. "Just hearing that because of Jesus I could be forgiven of everything I had ever done wrong, and that now I could make a fresh start, brought life to my bones," she writes.

Boyfriends had tossed Stormie aside, but Christ embraced her. He washed her sin-tarnished heart with His own blood. He filled her with hope and joy and peace. He transformed her into a woman of beauty and character through whom He is building His kingdom. Her books, including *The Power of a Praying Woman*, have sold more than 4.5 million copies and taught readers the principles of effective prayer.

We may feel tarnished and worthless, but that's not the way God sees us. He considers us His treasures. When we surrender our lives to Him, He cleanses us, restores us, and fulfills His purpose through us.

Perhaps we don't struggle with feeling worthless, but we know someone who does. If so, let's touch her life with God's love. A hug, an encouraging note, a cup of coffee, and a heart-to-heart talk can remind her that she's a treasure.

My prayer for you today, dear reader, is that God will impress truth upon you. May you live this day knowing that you're a woman of worth. You're beautiful. Highly valued. Treasured—by God Himself.

Inward Glimpse

Thank You, Father, for restoring broken lives. Make me aware of hurting women around me, and help me reach out in love. Amen.

- Read the hymn "Grace Greater than Our Sin." What does it mean to you?
- Do you know someone who feels tarnished? What can you do to encourage her?

Outward Glance

Father, I pray that You will guide _____ in Your truth and teach her Your ways. Remember Your great mercy and love but do not remember the sins of her youth. Instruct her in Your ways, for You are good and upright, and all Your ways are loving and faithful for those who keep the demands of Your covenant (Psalm 25:6-10). Amen.

One More Peek

I will rejoice in doing them good and will assuredly plant them in this land with all my heart and soul (Jeremiah 32:41).

Grace Greater than Our Sin

Julia H. Johnston

Marvelous grace of our loving Lord,
Grace that exceeds our sin and our guilt,
Yonder on Calvary's mount outpoured,
There where the blood of the Lamb was spilt.

Sin and despair like the sea waves cold,
Threaten the soul with infinite loss;
Grace that is greater, yes, grace untold,
Points to the Refuge, the mighty Cross.

Dark is the stain that we cannot hide,
What can avail to wash it away?
Look! there is flowing a crimson tide;
Whiter than snow you may be today.

Marvelous, infinite, matchless grace,
Freely bestowed on all who believe;
You that are longing to see His face,
Will you this moment His grace receive?

Grace, grace, God's grace,
Grace that will pardon and cleanse within;
Grace, grace, God's grace,
Grace that is greater than all our sin.

Practice Honor

Be devoted to one another in brotherly love.
Honor one another above yourselves.

Romans 12:10

Upward Gaze

Father, You are the King eternal, immortal, invisible, the only God (1 Timothy 1:17). To You belong honor and glory forever! I turn from other gods and honor Your name alone (Isaiah 26:13). Amen.

~

Clair maneuvered her grocery cart into the checkout line. A woman with a little girl, perhaps five or six years old, placed her purchases on the conveyor belt ahead of her. Eager to help, the girl reached into the cart and grabbed an egg carton. As she turned to place it on the belt, however, it slipped from her grasp and crashed to the floor. Eggs splattered and oozed from the carton.

"Can't you do anything right?" the woman growled. "Why don't you leave things alone?"

"It was an accident," the girl sputtered.

"Yeah, right," the woman said. "Just stand there and don't touch anything else. I don't need your help." The girl winced and stared at the spill.

Clair winced too. She felt the youngster's pain. *Poor thing*, she thought. *If this is the way her mother treats her in public, I wonder what it's like at home.*

Clair instinctively rushed to the child's rescue. She asked the checkout clerk for a roll of paper towels and said, "Not a problem. I'll clean this up in a jiffy." She smiled at the youngster. "I saw you trying to help. That was a kind thing to do. I'm sorry this accident happened."

The woman glowered and muttered a few unintelligible words. But the youngster's face lit up. She smiled shyly at Clair. "Can I help?" she asked.

"Of course," said Clair. She handed the girl a wad of paper towel and showed her how to pick up the slippery eggs. They completed their task in a few moments. "Well done," she said. The girl smiled again.

Clair watched the duo exit the store. "God, go with that child," she prayed. "Protect her from verbal and other abuse. And teach her mother the importance of demonstrating honor."

Honor—the act of showing respect or giving recognition to another. "When we honor someone, we regard him as a priceless treasure whether he feels valuable or not," says Dr. Gary Smalley. "When speaking about relationships, honor is foundational to all other skills. We can't enjoy successful, satisfying relationships without it."

Dr. Greg Smalley adds,

> Honoring someone means more than recognizing his inherent worth simply because he's created in God's image. It means giving him preference, considering him more valuable than myself. On a scale of one to ten, if I consider myself a 9.8, I treat him as 9.9. It's increasing the posture of humility by serving that other person.[6]

Whether we're enmeshed in difficult relationships or we want to strengthen healthy ones, we can remember Jesus' example. Rather than choosing to save His own life, He showed us honor by sacrificing it for us. His actions proved that He considered us as priceless treasures, more important than Himself.

As believers, we're to follow Christ's example. So how can we honor others in day-to-day living? Here are a few suggestions: We can set aside our work and look at our children and teens when they speak to us. We can forego personal convenience and give our spouse the gift of time to pursue a personal interest or develop a skill. We can forfeit a new outfit or a restaurant meal and use the money to send a less fortunate woman to a weekend retreat. We can give up a Saturday afternoon to watch a single mom's children.

These simple acts communicate honor. They show that we consider others more important than ourselves. Imagine, for a moment, how the world would be transformed if every man, woman, and child valued others as priceless treasures!

As individual women, we may not be able to turn the world upside down by honoring others. But we can set the example for our family and friends. And we can trust the Lord that as we show honor to those we love, He'll trigger a far-reaching ripple effect that strengthens countless relationships.

Inward Glimpse

Dear Father, thank You for demonstrating honor through Jesus' example. Make me aware of opportunities to demonstrate honor to those around me. Amen.

- List three ways to show honor to your immediate or extended family this week.
- If you've spoken hurtful words or displayed wrong behavior toward someone, ask his forgiveness. Ask the Lord to teach you how to show honor to that person.

Outward Glance

Lord, I pray that _____ will honor You not only with her lips but also with her heart (Matthew 15:8). And having been bought with the precious blood of Jesus, may she honor You with her body (1 Corinthians 6:20). May her lifestyle of honoring others bring You pleasure. Amen.

One More Peek

He who does not honor the Son does not honor the Father, who sent him (John 5:23).

God-Shaped Void

And God is able to make all grace abound to you,
so that in all things at all times, having all that you need,
you will abound in every good work.

2 CORINTHIANS 9:8

Upward Gaze

God, You are all I need. I've set You continually before me.
Because You're at my right hand, I will not be shaken (Psalm
16:8-11). You fill me with joy in Your presence! Amen.

~

You've probably heard the phrase "Mankind was created with a
God-shaped void." Because God wants a personal relationship with us,
He's placed within our hearts a vacuum that only He can fill.
Substituting Him with a human relationship, an object, personal goals,
or even a ministry doesn't work.

Wendy recently discovered this truth. For many years she'd enjoyed
a special closeness with her two daughters, whom she homeschooled.

But when the girls reached eighth and ninth grades, they wanted more involvement with peers and extracurriculars. They began attending public school, which naturally meant they spent less time at home. Wendy's relationship with her daughters shifted, leaving her feeling displaced and lonely.

Those feelings grew when her church restructured and eliminated her position. They compounded when she was overlooked for a committee for which she felt qualified. Other circumstances entered her life, and they too added to her discouragement.

During that time, Wendy had been leading a weekly Bible study. Although others considered her an excellent teacher, she began questioning her own ability. *What do I have to offer anyone?* She asked herself tough questions. *Who am I? Who is God, and what does He want from me?*

One Sunday morning, Wendy listened to a preacher explain Lamentations 3. Vivid word pictures described Jeremiah's emotions— "He has broken my teeth with gravel; he has trampled me in the dust…my soul is downcast within me (verses 16-20). Wendy identified with his despair.

But the pastor turned his focus. "Because of the LORD's great love we are not consumed, for his compassions never fail," he read. "They are new every morning; great is your faithfulness. I say to myself, 'The LORD is my portion; therefore I will wait for him.' The LORD is good to those whose hope is in him, to the one who seeks him; it is good to wait quietly for the salvation of the LORD" (verses 22-26).

Wendy had known those verses most of her life, but they'd never spoken as powerfully. Tears streamed down her face as she sensed the Lord saying, "I love you so much. Make Me your portion. Seek Me. I am enough."

At that point, she realized that she'd depended on her family rather than the Lord to fill her God-shaped void. She'd also sought the approval of others rather than being content with only the Lord's approval. Later, as she read her Bible at home, He reinforced His message through Psalm 37:4. "Delight yourself in the LORD"—not relationships, a ministry, or any other thing.

But God wasn't finished with Wendy yet. She received an assignment while attending a conference for Bible study leaders several weeks later. Using the study sheets provided, she reflected on God's Word and its life application. The suggested Scriptures were—you guessed it—Lamentations 3 and Psalm 37.

Again, God reassured Wendy of His love and directed her heart toward seeking Him only. Again, tears coursed down her cheeks. She ended her assignment with a written prayer—*God, You've spoken to me so clearly...I feel closer to You and Your love than I ever have. I feel broken and shattered but awed by Your love.* She left the conference resolved to fill her God-shaped void with only Him. She's never looked back.

In her book *Walking in Total God-Confidence,* Donna Partow writes that nothing apart from the Lord Himself will fulfill us.

> We have a hole in our heart the size of the Grand Canyon, so we hand our husband a bucket and say, "Here, you fill it." Or we hand it to our church, our friends, or what have you. We fail to realize that filling that hole is something only God can do. And he can only do it if we will let him.[7]

God longs for us to find our fulfillment in Him alone. He's created us with a vacuum that screams to be occupied. As Wendy discovered and Donna teaches, filling the void with relationships or service or whatever doesn't work. God alone is our portion. No substitute will do.

Inward Glimpse

Dear Father, thank You for wanting a relationship with me. Be my portion, my sufficiency every moment of every day. Amen.

- Have you tried to fill your God-shaped void with anything other than God? If so, what are those things?
- Write a prayer asking God to keep your heart true to Him alone.

Outward Glance

Father, I pray that _____ will find fulfillment in You alone. Teach her to delight herself in You rather than mere human relationships, the approval of others, or possessions (Psalm 37:4). Amen.

One More Peek

But I trust in your unfailing love;
    my heart rejoices in your salvation.
I will sing to the LORD,
    for he has been good to me (Psalm 13:5).

Humility

God opposes the proud but gives grace to the humble.

JAMES 4:6

Upward Gaze

Heavenly Father, who is like You? You arm me with strength and make my way perfect. With Your help I can advance against a troop; with You I can scale a wall (2 Samuel 22:30,33). You alone are the source of my strength and abilities. Amen.

～

In her PC (post-college, pre-children) days, Blair, a self-confessed techno geek, landed a great job selling business phone systems. She approached her new position puffed with pride. *I can do this!* she thought. *I've done sales before. I'm goooood.* But things didn't happen the way she'd anticipated.

Blair submitted one sales proposal after another, but to her shock, each received a resounding rejection. To make matters worse, circumstances beyond her control at the office waged war against her.

Her self-confidence dissipated, and her inability to secure sales jeopardized her job.

Blair's sales manager gave her a final chance to reverse her losing streak. Together they visited a mortgage company where Blair presented their product. She waited for a positive response. It never came.

As she returned to the office, Blair pondered her situation. She and her husband had recently purchased a house. They needed her income to pay the mortgage; losing her job would strain them financially. At the same time, however, she admitted that her attitude had been prideful. Could it be that God had arranged circumstances to get her attention?

God, if You don't want me to have this job, I understand, she prayed silently. *I've been really proud. Losing my job will hurt us financially, but I give it to You. Show me what to do next, and I'll do it.*

The next week, Blair's boss called her into his office and broke the news. "I'm sorry, but I'm letting you go. This job isn't working out." He paused then extended an offer she hadn't expected. "But we have another position that I think you'd do well in—programming the systems we're selling."

Blair could hardly wait to discuss the opportunity with her husband. Again, she felt confident that she could do the job and do it with excellence. But this time, she committed her work to the Lord and acknowledged Him as the source of her knowledge and abilities. Within two years, she moved back into sales. This time, she sold more than a million dollars worth of equipment in one year. What made the difference?

Her attitude makeover.

Rather than believing she could handle her job in her own strength as she had once believed, Blair acknowledged her dependence upon the Lord. After all, He sculpted her unique abilities and gave her a job to match them. He gave her a healthy body and a sound mind to do that job. And hey—He even provided the vehicle to drive to work each day! When she admitted her dependence upon Him, He blessed her in ways she never thought imaginable.

God wants us women to humble ourselves before Him, to admit our dependence upon Him. Wives and mothers, church secretaries, school teachers, engineers, lawyers, lifeguards, librarians, or whatever—if we approach our role puffed with pride and convinced that we're *goooood*, we may find ourselves being force-fed a big serving of humble pie.

But when we humble ourselves before the Lord, He smiles. When we acknowledge that everything we are and have comes from Him, He's pleased. I can almost hear Him say, "Smart move. Now let Me show you what I can do."

To keep ourselves from becoming puffed with pride, we can begin each day with a simple statement: "Father, I depend on You for everything, even my next breath." Doing so reminds us of His position as absolute Lord in our lives and frees Him to do what He wants in and through us. Is there any better way to live?

Inward Glimpse

Dear Father, thank You for reminding me that I'm dependent on You for everything. Keep me mindful of that truth so pride doesn't consume me. Amen.

- List areas in your life that are prone to make you prideful. Write a short prayer confessing your pride. Thank God for giving you those abilities and then give Him the freedom to use them in whatever ways He wishes.

- Besides your next breath, name those things for which you depend on God.

Outward Glance

Lord, please grant _____ a humble heart. May she pray and seek Your face and turn from her wicked ways. And when she does that, I pray that You will hear from heaven, forgive her sins, and heal her land (2 Chronicles 7:14). Amen.

One More Peek

Humble yourselves, therefore, under God's mighty hand, that he may lift you up in due time (1 Peter 5:6).

His Power for
the Big Stuff

*But he said to me, "My grace is sufficient for you,
for my power is made perfect in weakness."*

2 CORINTHIANS 12:9

Upward Gaze

Father, I praise You for arming me with strength and
making my way perfect (2 Samuel 22:33). You make me
more than a conqueror through Christ who loved me
enough to give His life on my behalf (Romans 8:37). Amen.

~

One morning, two years after I began writing seriously, I read a
newspaper headline: "Rescuer Recalls Fateful Night Over Cape Scott."
The account described a life-risking rescue at sea amid hurricane-force
winds.

This event contains all the elements of a drama-in-real-life story, I
thought. *Someone needs to write this for* Reader's Digest. *Won't be me,*

though. I don't have enough experience to investigate and pull it together. The mere thought tied my stomach in nervous knots.

I dialed the publication's Canadian headquarters. "Hello," a man's voice answered.

"Uh…is this *Reader's Digest?*"

"Yep. What can I do for you?"

"I think I know of a story you might want," I said. The man listened, asked a few questions, and then encouraged me to gather interviews and submit a proposal.

I pitched an excuse. "I'm too busy for this."

"You'd have several months to research and write it."

I hesitated. *Me? I can't do this.*

You're right. You can't, the Lord seemed to say. *But I can. Go ahead. Say yes and watch Me work.* I gulped. I sensed that this was a God-given assignment and obedience wasn't optional.

"Okay, I'll try," I said. "By the way, who are you?"

"The editor in chief," the man replied. I gulped again.

Pursuing that story meant locating the survivors, interviewing Coast Guard officers, and tracking police records. Because the accident claimed two men's lives, I spent an afternoon talking with a grieving widow and a brokenhearted fiancée. The entire process far outweighed my skills, but that didn't matter to God. When I obeyed His marching orders, He enabled me to successfully complete the task.

Scripture contains many stories of how God enabled people to fulfill tasks for which they weren't qualified. Take Gideon, for example. Year after year he witnessed the Midianites descend like swarms of locusts into Israel. They impoverished the Israelites and ravaged their crops. One afternoon, he received his orders: "Go in the strength you have and save Israel out of Midian's hand. Am I not sending you?" (Judges 6:14).

Gideon was no army general, and he knew it. He pitched an excuse: "But Lord, how can I save Israel? My clan is the weakest in Manasseh, and I am the least in my family."

And God replied, "Oh my goodness, you're right! What was I thinking? I'll change plans and find someone better equipped!"

No, He didn't! Not in my Bible! Rather, God said, "I will be with you, and you will strike down the Midianites as if they were but one man."

And that's exactly what happened. Gideon and his measly band of 300 men armed with—get this—trumpets and empty jars with torches inside trampled that locust-like army.

When God gives us assignments for which we feel unqualified, we can relax. He'll never ask us to perform a task without giving us what's needed to get the job done. He'll give us strength, wisdom, and finances. He'll rearrange schedules, put certain people in our path, and even coordinate the weather if needed.

Too often we analyze the assignment through our capabilities or lack thereof: *Teach Sunday school? Who, me? No way! I've never had any training.*

Write a letter to a government official protesting his stance on a particular issue? Who, me? I can't express myself eloquently!

Lead a support group? Are you kidding? I don't do public speaking.

Next time we face a task bigger than our abilities, let's focus on God's capabilities. And let's remember His words to Gideon: "I will be with you" (Judges 6:16). Like Gideon, we can obey God's marching orders and watch Him work.

Inward Glimpse

Dear Father, thank You for equipping me for the assignments You give. Help me focus on Your capabilities rather than my abilities or lack thereof, in Jesus' name. Amen.

- For what God-given assignment do you feel inadequate? Being a mother or ministry wife? Teaching a class? Leading a support group? Write a prayer thanking God that He'll provide whatever's necessary to get the job done.

- Judges 7:2-7 shows that God whittled Gideon's army from 22,000 men to 300 men "in order that Israel may not boast against me that her own strength has saved her." He wanted to receive the glory for the victory, so He made the odds of winning even more impossible. Have you ever faced a situation that looked impossible? How did He deliver you?

Outward Glance

Father, I pray that _____ will recognize her own inadequacy. May she speak not with her own wise words or persuasive speech. Rather, may her words and life demonstrate Your Spirit's enabling so others' faith might rest not on man's wisdom but on God's power (1 Corinthians 2:4-5). Amen.

One More Peek

But God chose the foolish things of the world to shame the wise; God chose the weak things of the world to shame the strong...so that no one may boast before him (1 Corinthians 1:27,29).

Dangerous Beauty

Now choose life, so that you and your children may live
and that you may love the LORD your God,
listen to his voice, and hold fast to him.

DEUTERONOMY 30:19-20

Upward Gaze

God, You've said that the fear of the Lord is the fountain of life, turning people from the snares of death (Proverbs 14:27). I praise You for being that life for me. Thank You for making the way for me to avoid trouble and hardship. Amen.

~

Morning sun smiled through Joy's windows and beckoned her outside. She opened the door and stepped into its warmth, but as she did, she realized something was wrong. Sparrows, goldfinches, chickadees, and a myriad of other birds usually visited the birdfeeders in her flower garden, filling the air with their chirps and trills. But today they were gone. Only silence remained.

Joy glanced around the yard. Her eyes fell on a peregrine falcon roosting in the apple tree. *Ah-ha,* thought Joy. *He frightened the little birds away.* She watched him for a few moments. *He's gorgeous. I'd love to enjoy his beauty all day.*

As she spoke, Joy realized the ramifications of her wish. Enjoying the falcon's beauty would mean sacrificing the other birds' presence and songs. The two couldn't coexist in the same yard. Which did she desire more?

What a vivid illustration of a life principle applicable to women of all ages and from all walks of life! Life presents us with choices every day. Some seem more attractive than others, but choosing them often means sacrificing something of eternal value.

Let me give an example or two. Physical beauty carries enormous weight in our society. Cosmetics advertisements convey the message that perfection is normal. They dupe us into believing that if our complexion or appearance is less than perfect, we're subpar.

The ads work. A recent *Time* magazine stated that 2.1 million cosmetic surgeries were performed in the United States in 1997. By 2003, that total escalated to 8.3 million—a 395 percent increase.[8]

What does the emphasis on physical appearance mean to us? It presents us with a choice. We can either jump aboard society's value train and pay big bucks for physical beauty, which eventually fades away, or we can embrace God's eternal values and focus on our inner beauty. There's nothing wrong with spending time and money on our appearance to accentuate what God's given us, but if our desire for physical attractiveness becomes our main focus, we sacrifice the impact God wants to make through us on those around us. The two values can't exist in the same heart. Which do we desire more?

Here's another example. Sometimes we feel like a plain little bird stuck in our environment. For some, that means cooking and cleaning and raising children. For others, it means waking up beside a spouse whose appeal died long ago, or spending eight hours each day doing the same job. Nothing exciting ever happens. Wouldn't a change be nice?

We flip through the television channels one morning. Gorgeous, successful soap opera stars lure us, and we stop to flirt with fantasy. Or we bury ourselves in romance novels to escape the mundane. Or we toy with the idea of having an affair. Impure thoughts provide escape from our confines.

We're faced with a choice: Give thanks in the midst of our circumstances and find our satisfaction in the person of Jesus Christ, or entertain impure thoughts that bring momentary fulfillment. Which do we desire more?

Choices confront us every day. Some flaunt a beauty that far exceeds others, but it's a dangerous beauty that costs us dearly in the end. Pursuing those options often requires sacrificing something that may seem less attractive or exciting at the moment but carries eternal value.

How can we remain single-minded, focused on what's close to God's heart? By maintaining and enjoying a close friendship with Him through Bible reading. By abiding in His presence as we speak with Him throughout our day. By filling our minds with His Word. Doing these things enables us to live victoriously with hearts pleasing to God.

Inward Glimpse

Dear Father, thank You for showing me the importance of choosing wisely. Keep my heart steadfast on You and Your ways. Amen.

- Describe a situation in which you were forced to choose between two conflicting values. What was the result of your choice?
- Ask God for discernment so you can tell when you're being attracted by a dangerous beauty.

Outward Glance

Father, I pray that _____ will walk in righteousness and know life (Proverbs 12:28). Teach her to incline her ear to

Your sayings, to keep them in her sight and in the midst of her heart, for they will be life to her (Proverbs 4:20-22). Amen.

One More Peek

There is a way that seems right to a man,
   but in the end it leads to death (Proverbs 14:12).

Hospitality

Offer hospitality to one another without grumbling.

1 PETER 4:9

Upward Gaze

Father, thank You for modeling servanthood through Jesus.
He did nothing out of selfish ambition but walked in
humility and considered others better than Himself. He set
aside His own comforts and looked to the interests of others
(Philippians 2:3-4). What an incredible example! Amen.

~

Ding-dong. Trish looked at the kitchen clock—5:45. Her dinner
guests were 15 minutes early. She wasn't quite ready, but that was okay.
She scraped the chopped tomatoes from the cutting board into the
salad bowl and walked down the hall to answer the door.

"Come in," said Trish. One by one, her guests—a mom, a dad, and
three kids—filed into the entryway. "Let me take your coats. So tell me,
are you settling in okay?"

"The bedrooms are ready for tonight, and we've almost finished unpacking the kitchen boxes," the woman replied. "Thank you for inviting us for dinner. We've had a long day. You're a life saver."

Trish smiled. She'd heard those words before. This wasn't the first time she'd invited new neighbors for a meal. Nor would it be the last. She loved practicing hospitality and making her home a place where others felt welcome.

A half hour later, the table was set and dinner was served. Trish dished up a surefire favorite—spaghetti, green salad, and garlic bread. She capped it with chocolate brownies.

"Thanks, Mom. Can we go play now?" asked her youngest, swiping his milk moustache with the back of his hand. "Sure—have a good time!" she said.

The kids dashed to the family room. The adults sipped coffee and became better acquainted. The evening ended when the neighbors decided they should unpack a few more boxes before time slipped away.

"Come again," said Trish as she handed them their coats. She returned to the kitchen, cleaned up the dirty dishes, and removed a package of hamburger buns from the freezer for tomorrow's lunch. Perhaps she could invite a family for barbecued burgers after church...

When you hear the word *hospitality*, what do you envision? Entertaining dinner guests with a gourmet meal served on fine china? Or extending a spontaneous invitation for soup and sandwiches? I prefer the latter. It's easy. And it's doable despite our busy lifestyles.

Trish feels the same way. She lives by the motto "Keep it simple, sweetie." And for good reason—she has three kids involved in various extracurricular activities, she volunteers in their school, and she works part-time outside her home.

Despite her busyness, Trish practices hospitality on a regular basis. She wants her home to be a place where others feel free to put their feet up and lay their worries down, a place from where they'll re-enter the world refreshed. She's doing a great job. And she makes it look so simple. Perhaps it's because she understands the difference between hospitality and entertaining.

Nearly 30 years ago, I bought a book entitled *Open Heart, Open Home* by Karen Burton Mains. In it, the author defines the difference:

Entertaining says, "I want to impress you with my beautiful home, my clever decorating, my gourmet cooking." Hospitality, however, seeks to minister. It says, "This home is not mine. It is truly a gift from my Master. I am His servant and I use it as He desires." Hospitality does not try to impress, but to *serve*.[9]

Entertaining binds. Hospitality frees. It puts people, not things, first. It doesn't care if guests see toys on the floor or splatters on the bathroom mirror. It allows people to put away false pretenses and be themselves. It provides shelter, a place of healing. And, according to Mains, it "does everything with no thought of reward, but takes pleasure in the joy of giving, doing, loving, serving."

By serving others, we model Christ. He came not to be served, to impress, or to seek esteem in others' eyes. Rather, He came to bless others with no thought of their repaying the favor. We can do the same.

In the midst of our busyness, we can bless others through hospitality by keeping it simple, sweetie. We can serve soup (make a *big* pot of homemade soup, serve half, and freeze the rest for last-minute invitations), rolls, cheese, and pickles. We can organize a neighborhood potluck. We can invite a family for popcorn and table games. We can include singles—young and old. On special occasions, like Christmas and Thanksgiving, we can include those who live far from family.

By serving others through hospitality, we give them opportunity to see Christ in us and feel His presence in our homes. And we receive joy in knowing that they're blessed.

Inward Glimpse

Dear Father, thank You for modeling servanthood. Help me see opportunities to serve others through practicing hospitality. Amen.

- List the things that hinder you from practicing hospitality.
- List three ways that you can serve others this month.

Outward Glance

Father, I pray that _____ will love others deeply. May she serve others in the strength You provide so that in all things God may be praised (1 Peter 4:8,11). Amen.

One More Peek

Be devoted to one another in brotherly love…share with God's people who are in need. Practice hospitality (Romans 12:10, 13).

Creative Genius

Upward Gaze

Father God, creation displays Your omnipotence. Your word made the heavens. The breath of Your mouth brought the starry host into being. You gather the sea into jars and the deep into storehouses (Psalm 33:6-7). Who among the gods is like You—majestic in holiness, awesome in glory, working wonders (Exodus 15:11)? You are exalted, Lord, above all else. Creation reflects Your magnificent power! Amen.

~

Some people are creative geniuses. Others are not. Once upon a time I thought I belonged to the first group. As a kid, I used my mom's sewing machine to create Barbie clothes. Let me be honest…these were *basic.* To me, a skirt was a piece of cloth folded in half and stitched down the side. Who needed a hem or waistband? A top was also a piece of cloth folded in half and stitched down the side. If Barbie was lucky, I sewed straps. If not, it didn't matter anyway…the top was so tight that it would never fall off.

When my daughters were toddlers, I thought I'd apply my seamstress skills to their wardrobe. You know, whip up a few frilly dresses, pants, and pajamas. I bought patterns, fabric, stickpins, a seam ripper, a gizmo that resembled a miniature pizza cutter, and other supplies that promised to help me sew like a pro.

Then reality struck and I realized my limitations. Someone told me that fabric needed a nap. Dots and arrows littered the patterns. My sewing machine jammed. Stickpins drew blood.

I completed a few kid-sized dresses that actually solicited compliments. But others nearly drove me to the brink with baffling buttonholes or zippers that were not only invisible—they were invincible too. I stitched for hours, but to my dismay, my efforts produced only lopsided armholes and crooked hemlines. No matter how hard I tried, my understanding and abilities weren't adequate for the task.

How unlike God, who possesses infinite understanding and abilities! He, the creative genius, spoke the world into being. No sweat, no stress, no mistakes. He carpeted the planet with trees and shrubs of every size and color. He sprinkled the earth with flowers—white daisies, yellow lupine, purple violets, red tulips, delicate baby's breath, and more. He filled the world with feathery birds, fuzzy critters, and finned sea creatures. He placed the sun, moon, and stars in their positions. He created and designed a plan for every man, woman, and child who ever existed. Now *that's* the evidence of a creative genius!

Some folks may actually be creative geniuses, but earth's best can't equal God's skills in that department. Creation reveals that He understands everything and can do anything. When a problem faces us, we can ask Him for wisdom, and He'll give it. When we're confused about what direction to take, we can ask Him for guidance, and He'll give that too. The same hand that spun the sky's cotton-candy clouds holds us when we hurt. The voice that spoke the world into existence calms the storm and whispers peace when we're afraid. We can admit our limitations and trust His understanding and abilities.

Inward Glimpse

Creator God, thank You for revealing Yourself through creation. Help me remember that Your power and understanding know no limits. Amen.

- Go for a walk and enjoy the beauty of God's creation. Look for intricacies such as symmetry in leaves and floral petal designs. Listen for different bird songs. Take a small child with you and see God's handiwork through his or her eyes.
- Read the hymn "This Is My Father's World." Meditate on its truths. What does this hymn teach you about God?

Outward Glance

Dear Father, because You're omnipotent, You're the perfect source of strength. May _____recognize Your power to answer prayer and do the impossible. When she feels inadequate or intimidated, impress upon her that she can do all things in Your strength (Philippians 4:13). May she see You riding the heavens to help her. May she recognize that You, the eternal God, are her refuge, and underneath are Your everlasting arms (Deuteronomy 33:25-27). Amen.

One More Peek

Let them praise the name of the LORD,
 for his name alone is exalted;
 his splendor is above the earth and the heavens
 (Psalm 148:13).

This Is My Father's World

Maltbie D. Babcock

This is my Father's world, and to my listening ears
All nature sings, and round me rings, the music of the spheres.
This is my Father's world: I rest me in the thought
Of rocks and trees, of skies and seas; His hand the wonders wrought.

This is my Father's world, the birds their carols raise,
The morning light, the lily white, declare their Maker's praise.
This is my Father's world: He shines in all that's fair;
In the rustling grass I hear Him pass, He speaks to me everywhere.

This is my Father's world, O let me ne'er forget
That though the wrong seems oft so strong, God is the Ruler yet.
This is my Father's world: The battle is not done;
Jesus who died shall be satisfied, and earth and heaven be one.

China Teacups

*There are different kinds of gifts, but the same Spirit. There are
different kinds of service, but the same Lord. There are different kinds
of working, but the same God works all of them in all men.*

1 CORINTHIANS 12:4-6

Upward Gaze

Father, Your deeds in man's behalf are awesome! May all the
earth worship You and sing praises to You (Psalm 66:4-5).
Amen.

~

Margaret Bayne hosts the *best* tea parties. Every summer during
family camp, our ministry founder's wife invites first-time attendees
to her garden. There, tucked under a lush green canopy, she sets a small
round table with delicate china cups of every color and description.

Purple violets and green leaves adorn one cup. Pink wild roses and
slender grasses decorate another. Gold filigree embellishes a third.
Yellow mums, lily-of-the-valley sprigs, an oriental garden scene—these

designs and more bring pleasure to those who sip the cups' steamy contents.

Each cup bears a different pattern. And Margaret's guests who enjoy the collection are equally unique. One woman introduces herself as a single mom with three children. "I've been on my own for five years," she says. "I'll tell you one thing for sure—single parenting is not for the fainthearted."

"I've been trying to start my own interior design business," says another. "It's something I've always wanted to do. The time seems right."

"My family recently returned from Taiwan," a third woman says, "but we won't stay in North America for long. Our work is calling us back."

"We've adopted two children this year," says a fourth. "Let's see— their arrival means we have a dozen kids at home!"

Sometimes the conversation deepens, and the women share their frustrations, their hopes, and their dreams. Occasionally they tell about their spiritual journey—where they've come from, where they're bound, and the bumps and detours they've encountered along the way. Like the teacups from which they sip, their stories are different from the others, and for good reason—each guest comes from a unique background and possesses her own blend of personality and abilities.

We women often compare ourselves to others. We admire our neighbor's intelligence. *I wish I could think quickly the way she does.* We envy another's musical inclinations. *It's not fair—she can play four musical instruments and sing. I can't even hum a simple tune.* We covet someone's physical appearance. *Silky skin, flawless figure—just like Barbie. And then there's me.* We watch another woman teach a Bible study—the same study we'd hoped to teach. Or we wish our life's journey was a little more exciting—like that new woman in town whose manner and clothes and car ooze glamour. Sometimes we adopt the attitude that says, *If only I could be just like so-and-so.*

We forget that God's hand has shaped us, and is continuing to shape us, into who He wants us to be for a reason. He has ordained a purpose for our lives, and that purpose carries eternal importance.

Would God achieve the same results if we were all identical? I doubt it. Imagine, for a moment, a church choir filled with gifted sopranos but no altos. Kiss harmony goodbye. Or a committee in which everyone wants to demonstrate their leadership skills. Uh-oh.

Rather than wishing we were just like someone else, we can give thanks for our individuality. Rather than being jealous or envious, we can thank God for the design He's stamped within others' lives, encourage them to use and develop their gifts, and cheer them on when they succeed.

When we fall into the comparison trap, we can remember that the beauty of Margaret's table setting lies in the teacups' variety. She could arrange her table using identical cups and saucers and it would still look attractive—in a uniform way. But the varied china cup collection adds character. And judging by the partygoers' oohs and aahs, the effect blesses everyone.

Inward Glimpse

Dear Father, thank You for stamping a unique design into my life. Help me to be content with what You've given me and to enjoy the variety You've created among women. Amen.

- Thank the Lord for creating you with your unique blend of personality, abilities, habits, and insight. If you struggle with feelings of inadequacy in a certain area, thank Him that He loves you anyway. Ask Him if you can improve that area in any way.

- How can you use your unique gifts and abilities to serve others?

Outward Glance

Father, I pray that You will be gracious to _____. Bless her and make Your face shine upon her. Bring honor to Yourself through the gifts and abilities You've given her so that Your ways may be known on the earth and Your salvation to all nations (Psalm 67:1-2). Amen.

One More Peek

But in fact God has arranged the parts in the body, every one of them, just as he wanted them to be (1 Corinthians 12:18).

Soul Survivor

Have no fear of sudden disaster
or of the ruin that overtakes the wicked,
for the LORD will be your confidence
and will keep your foot from being snared.

PROVERBS 3:25-26

Upward Gaze

God, I praise You because You preserve our lives and keep our feet from slipping. You test us, You refine us like silver. You lay burdens on our backs and bring us through fire and water. But You never abandon us. You bring us to a place of abundance (Psalm 66:9-12). Thank You! Amen.

~

Jeanne glanced around the hospital emergency room. *Family vacations shouldn't end here,* she thought. *But thank God, we survived.*

An hour earlier, Jeanne's family was driving along a remote mountain highway when an oncoming vehicle crossed the centerline. Jeanne's husband swerved right to prevent a head-on collision, but the other vehicle slammed into the side of their car.

Passersby offered rides to the nearest hospital, about a half-hour drive away. But the other driver, after giving his name and insurance information, insisted on staying by his disabled vehicle.

Now Jeanne held her 15-year-old son's hand as doctors checked his broken teeth and placed some 20 stitches on his face and eyelid. Her husband sat across the room, his jaw swelling as he waited for his X-ray results. Her uninjured 13-year-old daughter huddled on a couch in the staff lounge.

Several hours later, two state troopers entered the ER. "We found evidence of the other driver's drinking," one reported. They described the other vehicle's strong liquor stench. They also found empty beer cans, and the brand matched an hours-old sales receipt. But the driver was gone when they arrived, ending chances for a crucial sobriety test.

The troopers' report added distress to injury. *God, where are You in this situation?* Jeanne wondered. *And what are You doing through it?*

Throughout the following year, each family member's health suffered. Jeanne's stress, compounded by caring for her cancer-stricken mother-in-law, translated into physical problems: hair loss, migraine headaches, and panic attacks when she tried to play her violin in public—an activity she'd once enjoyed.

Though spiritual dryness threatened, Jeanne persevered in reading her Bible and praying. She wanted to view her circumstances through God's eyes, to regard the situation with His insight and wisdom. One day, while reading Proverbs 3, she paused at verses 25 and 26—today's key verses. She thought of her family's sudden disaster and of the drunk driver's spiritual ruin. She acknowledged the Lord as her confidence through an uncertain future. But the last phrase puzzled her. *The Lord will keep my foot from being snared? What does that mean?*

Then the light dawned. *My attitude!* she thought. *My angry, bitter attitude toward the drunk driver could grip me in its trap. But God has promised to keep that from happening. How will He do that?*

Jeanne pondered that Scripture verse for five years. One morning she noticed a two-inch article in her local newspaper. A nonprofit organization devoted to educating impaired drivers wanted survivors of drunk driving accidents to tell their stories. She clipped the article and prayed about it, and then she called the panel moderator to offer her services.

Today, Jeanne speaks monthly to an average of 50 people convicted of "driving under the influence." She feels no anger. Rather, she understands the ruin they face—eternity without Jesus. She tells them her family's experience and encourages them to fill their heart's God-shaped vacuum with God Himself rather than liquor.

Introduced as a survivor, Jeanne gives thanks that the accident didn't claim her family members' lives. But she's a soul survivor too. In the face of adversity, she made the Lord her confidence. And when she did, God kept her from being snared by the enemy of anger and bitterness.

Have you ever faced sudden disaster? Perhaps a job layoff or a doctor's frightening diagnosis. Maybe a grown child's decision to blatantly walk away from his faith or a loved one's unexpected death. Sooner or later, everyone encounters it in one form or another.

When our turn comes, we can remember God's promise to be our confidence and to keep our foot from being snared. No matter what circumstances we encounter, we can walk in freedom as soul survivors.

Inward Glimpse

Dear Father, thank You for promising to be my confidence and to keep my foot from being snared. Remind me of this truth when sudden disaster strikes. Amen.

- What traps might snare your foot when adversity strikes unexpectedly?
- Write today's key verse on a 3 x 5 card and memorize it.

Outward Glance

Father, when _____ faces sudden disaster, I pray that You will turn her wailing into dancing. Remove her sackcloth and clothe her with joy that her heart may sing to You and not be silent (Psalm 30:11). Amen.

One More Peek

The righteous cry out, and the LORD hears them;
he delivers them from all their troubles (Psalm 34:17).

Agendas

"My thoughts are not your thoughts,
neither are your ways my ways,"
declares the LORD.

ISAIAH 55:8

Upward Gaze

Heavenly Father, I praise You for being all-wise. Your thoughts are not mine. Neither are Your ways my ways. As the heavens are higher than the earth, so are Your ways higher than mine and Your thoughts than mine (Isaiah 55:8-9). I rest in the knowledge of Your wisdom and sovereignty over all. Amen.

~

Agenda: a list or plan of things to be done or accomplished. According to the dictionary definition, that's what I had during the last week of August.

Our eldest daughter, Stephanie, would be attending Bible college about 1000 miles from home. She was to arrive on campus on

September first. Because my husband's ministry at a Christian camp required his presence during that time, Stephanie and I anticipated making the long trip by ourselves.

Perfect! I thought. *A great opportunity for quality mother-daughter time.* I began making plans: Drive through the Rocky Mountains. Buy freshly picked cherries and peaches along the way. Listen to Stephanie's favorite CDs. Stop for cold drinks whenever we feel like it. Spend a night at a hotel with a hot tub and swimming pool. Spend three days visiting my parents, and arrive at the college on the appointed day.

My plan seemed like a great send-off for Stephanie. But it lent appeal for another reason: The busy summer had exhausted me. I needed a holiday, and this would be it.

Stephanie's departure day arrived. We loaded the car with her belongings, waved goodbye to her dad and younger sister, and caught the ferry to the nearest town. Before we even reached the highway, however, my agenda blew to smithereens.

A traffic light turned red. We stopped. The light turned green. I stepped on the gas pedal. Nothing happened. I tried again.

Screech! The car lurched forward, its tires leaving rubber residue on the road. "What on earth was that?" I wondered aloud.

Stephanie stared. Her eyes registered shock. "Mom! I didn't know you could drive like that!"

"Like what?"

"Like a teenage guy," she said, obviously impressed with my skill.

Another red light. Another green. More rubber. Stephanie stared wide-eyed but said nothing this time. My heart hammered as we screeched and lurched our way to an auto repair shop.

The diagnosis? A nearly dead transmission. "The car will be ready in three days," said the mechanic.

Three days? I heard his words but didn't want to believe them. How could this happen? We'd still make the trip, but now it would be rushed, like the entire summer had been. I determined to remain positive in Stephanie's presence, but the tears flowed in private as I poured out my heart to the Lord. *I don't understand why You allowed this to happen. I wanted to spend relaxed time with my daughter before she left for college—is that too much to ask? I'm tired. I need a rest. Is that a selfish request?* I clutched my plans like a little kid squeezing a favorite toy, and cried, *Mine!*

I'll admit it. I let my disappointment dictate my response—I threw a three-day pity party, and the only guest was me. During that time, God performed a repair job in my heart. *Will you trust Me despite the change in plans?* He asked. *Will you give thanks even though your agenda fizzled?*

I thought of God's faithfulness and sovereignty and power. He knew the transmission would fail that day, and He could have prevented it. But for some reason, He chose not to do so. He had a different agenda—one that I might never understand. But He wanted me to embrace it and to give thanks even though I didn't appreciate it.

No doubt you've experienced situations in which your plans vaporized and you felt keenly disappointed. Perhaps your husband's job required his transfer to another city, but your house didn't sell before he left. You and the kids are left behind until someone buys it. Maybe a home business didn't develop as you'd planned, and now you're experiencing financial difficulties. Perhaps you'd planned goals for the women's ministry, but nothing's happening as you'd envisioned.

When our agenda fizzles despite our best efforts, we can choose to throw a pity party (believe me, it's lonely), or we can choose to thank the Lord for controlling our circumstances and making no mistakes. Releasing our plans and embracing His allows us to walk in freedom and confidence. Even when we don't understand why things happen as they do, we can rest in the knowledge that He loves us more than words can say, and He has our best in mind.

Inward Glimpse

Father, thank You for designing the perfect agenda for me. Help me accept it and trust You as You fulfill it. Amen.

- Describe an instance when you realized that your agenda didn't match the Lord's. How did you respond?
- Write today's key verse on a 3 x 5 card and memorize it.

Outward Glance

Father, I pray that _____ will embrace Your plans for each new day. Help her remember that You are her Father. Remind her that she is the clay and You are the potter, and she is the work of Your hands (Isaiah 64:8). Amen.

One More Peek

There is no wisdom, no insight, no plan
   that can succeed against the LORD (Proverbs 21:30).

Not Rejected

I said, "You are my servant";
I have chosen you and have not rejected you.

ISAIAH 41:9

Upward Gaze

Father, I will always have hope. I will praise You more and more. My mouth will tell of Your righteousness and of Your salvation all day long, even though I don't know its full measure. I will proclaim Your mighty acts, O Sovereign Lord (Psalm 71:14-16). Amen.

~

Our family visited Disneyland when our youngest child, Kim, was four years old. We'd enjoyed a half-dozen rides and were preparing to board another when a park employee pointed in Kim's direction. "I don't think she's tall enough," he said. "Put her against the measuring stick." Sure enough. Kim was two inches too short. "I'm sorry," he said. "She'll have to wait here."

Kim's chin quivered as she watched her dad and siblings board the ride and leave the platform. There she stood—set aside and feeling rejected as others moved on without her.

Perhaps you can identify. One minute everything's fine. The next instant, circumstances set you aside and leave you feeling rejected while others carry on without you.

That's what happened to Beryl. Her experience began with a phone call that told of her father-in-law's death several provinces away. The family budget could afford only one airline ticket, so she and her husband decided he would attend the funeral while she stayed home.

Beryl raced to the airport to make travel arrangements, but as she strode toward the terminal, she tripped over a curb and crashed to the concrete. She sustained a fractured arm and torn ligaments in her wrist and shoulder. An ambulance transported her to the hospital, but because her husband hoped to catch a standby seat on the next flight, he couldn't accompany her.

At home the next afternoon, Beryl stared at the sling-like contraption cradling her right arm. *How am I supposed to feed myself, and write phone messages, and bathe, and journal?* she wondered. She muddled through the next eight days, feeling rejected and alone.

Less than three weeks later, a company several thousand miles away offered Beryl and her husband a job. The opportunity meant leaving everything familiar behind, but they accepted and made the move. Before long, Beryl realized that her husband had come into a prominent position, but she had not.

Once again Beryl felt rejected. Now she battled feelings of inferiority. *Is something wrong with me?* she wondered. *Why am I always left behind?* Her arm still ached, and now her soul ached too. *Has God tossed me aside?* she wondered. *Has He thrown me away?*

She expressed her thoughts to God and immersed herself in His Word as she awaited His reply. He answered by directing her to Isaiah 41:9-10: "I said, 'You are my servant'; I have chosen you and have not rejected you. So do not fear, for I am with you; do not be dismayed, for I am your God. I will strengthen you and help you; I will uphold you with my righteous right hand."

The Scripture changed Beryl's perspective. The verses reminded her that regardless of her feelings, God loved and valued her. Even though she felt alone at times, His presence walked with her. She could greet each day with confidence, knowing that He held her life in His hands and could even use negative events to accomplish His desires.

The Old Testament character Joseph understood the same truth. If anyone had reason to believe he'd been rejected, he did. First, his brothers sold him into slavery. Later, when his master's wife falsely accused him of sexual assault, he landed in prison.

Had God tossed him aside? It certainly appeared so. There Joseph sat, alone behind bars. But Scripture says, "While Joseph was there in the prison, the LORD was with him; he showed him kindness and granted him favor in the eyes of the prison warden" (Genesis 39:20-21). God never left his side. And because He held Joseph's life in His hand, He used those negative circumstances to accomplish His purposes.

The same truth applies to us. No matter what situations we face, we can remember God's sovereignty and promised presence. Rather than entertaining thoughts of being rejected, we can fill our minds with the truth that God has chosen us and upholds us in His hand.

Inward Glimpse

Dear Father, thank You for choosing me and not rejecting me. When I'm feeling set aside, help me remember that You hold my life in Your hands. Amen.

- Describe a situation that left you feeling rejected. How did you respond? What did you learn through it?
- Write a short prayer thanking God that He holds you in His hand.

Outward Glance

Father, when _____ encounters circumstances that leave her feeling lonely and rejected, keep her focus on You. At those times, remind her that You have chosen her out of all the people on the face of the earth to be Your daughter, Your treasured possession (Deuteronomy 7:6). Amen.

One More Peek

You intended to harm me, but God intended it for good to accomplish what is now being done, the saving of many lives (Genesis 50:20).

Quiet Moments

Upward Gaze

Father, my soul finds rest in You alone. My salvation comes from You. You alone are my rock and my salvation. You're my fortress; I will never be shaken (Psalm 62:1-2). Amen.

~

Jeanette volunteered to cook for a week at the summer camp where she'd registered her oldest son. While there, she spent her days baking and preparing meals, and her evenings doing whatever she pleased. For the third consecutive evening, she settled into a lawn chair and opened a novel.

Aaaahh…bliss! she thought. *At home, I can only dream of doing this.* She recalled her last month's schedule and shook her head. *No wonder cooking for 150 campers feels like a vacation to me!*

Class parties and carpooling had cluttered Jeanette's calendar during the last month of school. When school ended, her church's annual five-day soccer camp began. She coached, led the worship sessions, and helped host a windup barbecue for the soccer players and their parents.

When the next Monday morning dawned, she loaded her three boys into the family vehicle and drove to a friend's house where she helped lead a vacation Bible school for five days. The following weekend brought invitations to five barbecues for various functions. And somewhere in the busyness, Jeanette celebrated her wedding anniversary and canned 21 quarts of cherries.

Jeanette arrived at the camp exhausted and wondering how she'd cope in the kitchen. Her worries eased when the cook explained the schedule. She took advantage of every free minute, relishing quiet reflective time on the lodge's deck. She reveled in the novelty of visiting with new friends and reading a book uninterrupted. And she chose to relax without feeling guilty!

When the week ended, Jeanette felt rested physically and refreshed mentally, spiritually, and emotionally. The respite sent her home better equipped to parent her busy boys with more patience, more love, and a renewed sense of humor.

Fortunate woman, eh? Not many of us have the freedom or luxury of doing what she did, but most women need a break. We lead hectic lifestyles—working in and outside our homes, serving on committees, maintaining a yard and house, spending time with family and friends, and raising children.

Too often we feel guilty for not accomplishing everything on our daily to-do list. Stress and fatigue drain the joy from our spirits, and before long, we're snippin' and snappin' at whoever crosses our path. If we're not careful, we go from being *busy* to *broken*.

Jesus understood the importance of drawing apart to prevent falling apart. A typical day found Him teaching in the synagogue, casting out demons, and healing the sick. On one occasion, an entire city gathered at His door, waiting for Him to minister to the needy (Mark 1:21-34). In the midst of His busyness, Jesus escaped to a mountain alone or with several disciples. Scripture also says that "very early in the morning, while it was still dark, Jesus got up, left the house and went off to a solitary place, where he prayed" (Mark 1:35). Then He went out and ministered again.

If Jesus sought times of refreshing, so should we! And we shouldn't feel guilty doing so. We might not have the freedom to trade home and family responsibilities for a weeklong solitary retreat, but we can take mini-breaks.

We can rest on the couch for 15 minutes while the kids play. We can sip tea while sitting on the back porch or read for 30 minutes before falling asleep at night. We can exchange child care one afternoon a month—not to catch up on unfinished projects but to spend three or four hours pursuing a hobby or taking a walk.

Note that Jesus' quiet time included prayer. He drew strength for His work through communion with His heavenly Father. The same principle applies to us. Regular time communing with God strengthens us for our tasks. It helps keep our perspective right. Those quiet moments in His presence keep us healthy and refreshed so that we might best reflect His love to those with whom we have contact every day.

Inward Glimpse

Dear Father, thank You for showing me that it's okay and necessary to seek quiet moments in Your presence. Help me do so consistently. Amen.

- Do you draw apart from your busyness to rest and be refreshed? If not, what hinders you from doing so?
- Set a reasonable goal for establishing a habit of drawing apart for renewal. Ask for help from a friend or family member if necessary.

Outward Glance

Father, I pray that in the midst of her activities, _____ will wait for You and put her hope in Your Word. May her soul wait for You more than watchmen wait for the morning (Psalm 130:5-6). And as she waits, refresh her with a renewed sense of Your glorious presence in her life. Amen.

One More Peek

But those who hope in the LORD
*   will renew their strength.*
They will soar on wings like eagles;
*   they will run and not grow weary,*
*   they will walk and not be faint (Isaiah 40:31).*

The Light

*When Jesus spoke again to the people, he said,
"I am the light of the world. Whoever follows me will never
walk in darkness, but will have the light of life."*

JOHN 8:12

Upward Gaze

Father, I praise You for revealing Yourself to us through Christ, the Light of the World. In Him was life, and that life is the light of men (John 1:4). Thank You for loving mankind enough to provide us with the life-giving Light. Amen.

∾

Light—we take it for granted, but without it, we'd be in big trouble. My encyclopedia states a few interesting facts:

Without light, we'd have to eliminate food from our menus. That's because green plants need sunlight to grow and produce food. All food comes from plants or from animals that eat them. So forget the steak and salad—and all other food for that matter.

Without light, we'd no longer see. Light that comes to our eyes makes seeing possible. Lose light, and the world's strongest eyeglasses won't restore our vision.

Without light, the world would be too cold to live. Woodstoves wouldn't help heat our homes because they need wood. And wood comes from plants, but plants don't grow without light.

Without light, we'd have no air to breathe. That's because plants give off oxygen. No light...no plants...no oxygen...uh-oh—no life.

Get the picture? Light gives life. Lest we doubt, we can perform a simple experiment: Shut a houseplant in a closet. Water it. Talk to it. Do whatever you want, but don't give it light. You don't have to be a horticulturalist to predict its fate.

Keeping these facts in mind, consider the significance of Jesus' proclamation: "I am the light of the world" (John 8:12). Basically, His statement means that He is the source and sustainer of all life, physical and spiritual.

Janine discovered this truth several years ago. Raised by her mother—a woman suffering from mental illness—she endured endless physical and verbal abuse. When she turned 14, she began dating a 19-year-old with a taste for beer and marijuana and pretty girls.

Janine's life pursued a downward spiral. At age 17, she quit school and hit the streets to support her drug addiction. Life grew darker and darker. Two years later, she attempted suicide. Thankfully, she failed. On her twenty-first birthday, she stood shivering on her all-too-familiar street corner. A stranger carrying a thermos approached her.

"Would you like some hot chocolate?" the woman asked. Janine eyed her with suspicion. The woman sensed her hesitation. "It's okay," she said. "I'm not going to hurt you. I want to help."

Janine had never heard those words expressed. She accepted the hot drink and listened as the woman spoke of Jesus' love for her. She also accepted a pamphlet with a phone number for a women's safe house.

Several weeks later, Janine pulled the crumpled pamphlet from her jeans pocket and dialed the number. That action triggered a series of events that rescued her from certain destruction and introduced her to a personal relationship with Jesus Christ. His presence shone life-giving light into her sin-darkened heart. His words illuminated her path so she could see and understand its dangers and ultimate destination, and they revealed a better road.

When Janine recalls the night she prayed to receive God's free gift of salvation, she says, "For the first time, I saw light at the end of the dark tunnel of my life. Jesus was that light." Amen, sister!

Once we establish a relationship with Christ, we have a responsibility to reflect His light to those around us, as the stranger did with Janine. Mother Teresa said, "Christians are the light for everyone else, for the whole world. If we are Christians, we must look like Christ. We must be like Him." She's right. By speaking kind words, modeling holy (not holier-than-thou) lives, and defending truth and righteousness, we reflect Christ's life-giving light to those with whom we associate every day.

When others watch us, I pray they'll see Christ. And may we, through word and deed, be faithful to present Him as the source and sustainer of our lives.

Inward Glimpse

Dear Father, thank You for sending the true light into the world. Fill my life with the light of His presence. Amen.

- Matthew 5:14,16 says, "You are the light of the world.... Let your light shine before men, that they may see your good deeds and praise your Father in heaven." List several practical ways that you can let your light shine before those around you.
- Read the hymn "The Light of the World Is Jesus." How has Jesus shone like a light into your life?

Outward Glance

Father, I pray that _____ will be a light in the world. Cause her life to be like a city high atop a hill, unable to be hidden. Cause her to give light to everyone she meets. May she let her light shine before others so they may see her good deeds and praise You (Matthew 5:14-16). Amen.

One More Peek

The city does not need the sun or the moon to shine on it, for the glory of God gives it light, and the Lamb is its lamp (Revelation 21:23).

The Light of the World Is Jesus

Philip P. Bliss

The whole world was lost in the darkness of sin;
The Light of the world is Jesus;
Like sunshine at noonday His glory shone in.
The Light of the world is Jesus.

No darkness have we who in Jesus abide;
The Light of the world is Jesus;
We walk in the Light when we follow our Guide.
The Light of the world is Jesus.

Ye dwellers in darkness with sin-blinded eyes,
The Light of the world is Jesus;
Go, wash at His bidding, and light will arise.
The Light of the world is Jesus.

No need of the sunlight in heaven, we're told;
The Light of the world is Jesus.
The Lamb is the Light in the city of gold.
The Light of the world is Jesus.

Come to the Light, 'tis shining for thee;
Sweetly the Light has dawned upon me;
Once I was blind, but now I can see;
The Light of the world is Jesus.

Pruning

I am the true vine, and my Father is the gardener.
He cuts off every branch in me that bears no fruit, while every branch
that does bear fruit he prunes so that it will be even more fruitful.

JOHN 15:1-2

Upward Gaze

Father, I praise You as the gardener in my life (John 15:1).
Thank You for pruning me to produce fruit (John 15:1-2).
I will sing of Your love forever. I will make Your faithful-
ness known through all generations (Psalm 89:1). Amen.

~

Our yard looks like a mini-orchard. Two apple trees produce
enough fruit to make approximately 30 quarts of homemade juice and
20 quarts of pie filling. A peach tree and a plum tree provide the mak-
ings for yummy jams. Raspberries and grapes yield juice and jellies (or
raccoon and deer snacks, if the critters eat the clusters before we can
pick them).

Gene and I have learned by experience that pruning influences the plants' production. After Gene snips the "suckers"—branches that draw energy from the tree but produce nothing—the plants appear delimbed and bare. The process pays off, however, and the harvest increases. We share our abundance with friends and preserve fruit for the winter months.

My friend Barb grows kiwifruit. An average tree in her orchard yields 600 to 800 kiwis each year, but that doesn't happen by accident. She pays close attention to the vines' growth.

Barb encourages a healthy harvest by "tip pruning." She pinches off the vines' young tips, forcing the plant to use its energy to produce fruit rather than simply grow long vines. She also removes dead branches and pulls young shoots that grow from the main trunk or from the ground. They, too, sap energy from the main vine and hinder the harvest.

In his book *Secrets of the Vine*, author Bruce Wilkinson says that God uses the same strategy to coax a more plentiful harvest from us. If our lives bear only a small amount of spiritual fruit, He wants to increase production. "His plan is to prune, which means to thin, to reduce, to cut off. As unthinkable as it sounds—as contradictory as it is—the Vinedresser's secret for more is…less."

Sometimes our lives, like rapidly growing trees and vines, produce suckers and tips. We fill our hours with activities and commitments that make us appear productive but in reality are nearly fruitless. God, the Master Gardener, wants to develop our full potential. How does He do that? According to Wilkinson, He "asks you to let go of things that keep you from His kingdom and your ultimate good."

In Sheryl's situation, pruning included cutting back the amount of time she spent in church activities. She'd acknowledged Christ as her Savior several years after she and Jon married. When she asked Jon to attend church with her, he refused. "I don't mind if you go, but don't expect me to," he said. "I'd rather stay home."

Before long, Sheryl joined two committees and choir. She spent more evenings at church than at home. That's when the pruning began. Jon grew unhappy with Sheryl's absence and asked her to make changes so they could spend evenings together. Although Sheryl valued time with her Christian friends, she loved her husband more and didn't want her activities to strain her marriage.

Sheryl solved the conflict by resigning from both committees and asking Jon if she could open their home to a weekly couples' Bible study. He agreed. Several weeks later, after meeting his wife's friends and participating in the study, he chose to follow Christ. Pruning resulted in greater abundance, but Sheryl had to release her own wants before that could happen.

Sometimes the pruning process feels more like hacking than careful, precise cutting. We wonder if God really loves us, and if so, why He can't use a less painful method to achieve His purposes. At those times, He asks us to trust Him. He knows exactly what must be done to yield the greatest spiritual harvest, and He doesn't make mistakes. Never, in history's entirety, has He snipped unnecessarily and exclaimed, "Oops! I goofed on that branch!"

When we recognize God's pruning in our lives, we can relax. His work won't strip our lives. Rather, it will make them better, richer, more abundant. We simply have to trust!

Inward Glimpse

Dear Father, thank You for pruning my life to produce abundant fruit. Help me accept it as for my good. Amen.

- When God prunes our lives, He asks us to let go of something that's keeping us from His kingdom and our ultimate good. What might He want to prune from your life?

- Would you like God to prune the unnecessary and fruitless preoccupations from your life? If so, give Him permission now.

Outward Glance

Father, I pray that _____ will remain in You and You in her. As a result of that relationship, grant that her life will bear much fruit. Remind her that apart from You, she can do nothing (John 15:4-5). Amen.

One More Peek

This is to my Father's glory, that you bear much fruit, showing yourselves to be my disciples (John 15:8).

Wait!

The LORD is good to those whose hope is in him,
to the one who seeks him;
it is good to wait quietly
for the salvation of the LORD.

LAMENTATIONS 3:25-26

Upward Gaze

Father, You are good and upright (Psalm 25:8). Yours eyes are on those who fear You, on those whose hope is in Your unfailing love. I wait in hope for You, for You are my help and my shield. My heart rejoices in You, for I trust in Your holy name (Psalm 33:18-21). Amen.

∾

Have you ever waited a l-o-o-o-n-g time for something you deeply desired? Maybe a marriage proposal. A much-needed vacation. A loved one's personal salvation. Reconciliation for a broken relationship. Healing from chronic illness. Conception or adoption.

If you have, you'll know waiting is not easy. In fact, sometimes we feel like *wait* is nothing more than a nasty four-letter word. That perspective, however, plants seeds that sprout into crankiness and impatience.

In his book *Waiting on God*, Andrew Murray shares valuable insights about waiting. He says that we often set our hearts upon the blessings for which we wait, but God wants us to think bigger:

> We were seeking gifts; He, the Giver, longs to give Himself and to satisfy the soul with His goodness. It is just for this reason that He often withholds the gifts, and that the time of waiting is made so long. He is all the time seeking to win the heart of His child for Himself. He wishes that we should not only say, when He bestows the gift, How good is God! but that long ere it comes, and even if it never comes, we should all the time be experiencing: It is *good* that a man should quietly wait: "The Lord is *good* to them that wait for him."[10]

In other words, He wants our longing to be for Him, not the blessings we seek. He wants us to say, in all sincerity, that He is good regardless of whether or not that much-longed-for thing becomes reality.

My friend Jan has been learning this. She and her family lived in South Africa from 1989 to 1991. In 1994 they volunteered at a mission hospital in Gabon. She loved the people, the culture, the experience, and the sense of making a positive, eternal impact on a needy land. Their term ended all too soon. They returned to Canada, but part of Jan's heart remained on the African continent.

I met Jan in 1998. As our friendship grew, she told me of her desire to return. But, being a married woman with two teenage sons, she knew her dream could not be fulfilled unless her family also wanted to invest directly into the lives of the African people.

Jan waited and prayed. During that time, she refused to push her family into doing what she wished. Instead, she supported them in their work and school, and she remained faithful to her commitments outside the home. Circumstances changed a few months ago. In August, 2004, she and her family traded Canada for Kenya.

Was waiting easy? Not at all. But the process enriched Jan's spiritual life, bringing her to a place of complete submission to God's will and total satisfaction with His goodness regardless of whether or not Africa played a role.

Jan and I spoke by phone recently. Her excitement bubbled as she told me the latest news. "Grace, everything's falling into place! Without even advertising our house, one of our kids' schoolteachers asked if he could rent it while we're away. Our oldest son will find a job and board with that family. And a friend volunteered to keep our dog!" We laughed together, marveling at God's faithfulness and rejoicing in His goodness.

Andrew Murray summarizes waiting in these words:

> What a blessed life the life of waiting then becomes, the continual worship of faith, adoring and trusting His goodness. As the soul learns its secret, every act or exercise of waiting just becomes a quiet entering into the goodness of God, to let it do its blessed work and satisfy our every need.[11]

As you wait, may your heart be directed into that continual "worship of faith." And may you be overwhelmed with His goodness every moment of every day!

Inward Glimpse

Father, thank You for lavishing Your goodness on me. Help me view waiting as an opportunity to know You more intimately rather than a hindrance to my plans. Amen.

- Describe a situation in which you waited on the Lord for direction, for provision, for wisdom, or whatever. How did you grow spiritually through that time?

- Write a short prayer asking the Lord to develop in you a continual "worship of faith" no matter what your circumstances.

Outward Glance

Lord, teach _____ to put her hope in Your Word. And teach her soul not only to wait for Your blessings, but to wait for You and Your goodness more eagerly than the watchmen wait for the morning (Psalm 130:5-6). Amen.

One More Peek

Wait for the LORD;
be strong and take heart
and wait for the LORD (Psalm 27:14).

Wrestle or Nestle?

Come to me, all you who are weary and burdened,
and I will give you rest.

MATTHEW 11:28

Upward Gaze

God, I praise You because You are my rock and salvation.
You are my fortress; I will never be shaken. My soul finds
rest in You alone (Psalm 62:1-2). Amen.

∽

Amy recently returned from eight months in Kenya, where she and
her husband, both medical doctors, worked in a mission hospital.
She'd lived overseas before, so she anticipated a smooth transition back
into North American life. But things didn't happen as she expected.

Amy sunk into a mental malaise. Simple tasks that required
thinking—reading, writing letters, answering e-mails, talking on the
phone—became impossible. She cried about nothing in particular for
at least an hour each day, and she felt angry at herself for being unable

to handle the busy schedule she'd always kept. *What's happening, God? Why can't I cope like I've always been able to?* she wondered.

The malaise lasted about two months. During the darkest two week period, Amy cried out to God, longing for deliverance from her anguish. "I'm Your child! I'm Yours completely. Whatever You want from me, I'm willing. Just tell me what You want me to do." She heard only silence. She searched the Psalms in an easy-to-understand translation but could neither sense God speaking nor remember what she'd read.

Finally, realizing she needed help, Amy told church friends about her struggle. They began praying for her. She sought her pastor's counsel—because of a similar experience, he understood her feelings. "I think this is a matter of learning to rest in the Lord," he said. "Whatever process is happening, let it happen."

His words resonated with Amy. As a doctor, she realized the importance of postoperative rest. "Don't push yourself," she advised her patients. "If something rips or stretches, you might not heal properly." Now it was her turn. She felt as though she'd undergone mental surgery and the pastor's advice, like a doctor's counsel to a patient, gave her permission to do nothing but wait.

Amy also recalled a story she'd heard while in Kenya. A five-foot, eight-inch, 150-pound fellow had taken a water lifesaving course. One day he had to "rescue" his six-foot, three-inch, 220-pound instructor. At first, the instructor thrashed and flailed, making it impossible for the student to move him. Finally he approached the teacher from behind, locked his arms, and held him underwater until he stopped struggling. Only then was he able to "save" him.

I've been thrashing like the instructor, thought Amy. *It's as though God has pushed me underwater because He wants me to stop fighting Him, to rest and trust whatever He's doing in my life. Don't wrestle, just nestle.* And that's what she finally did.

Amy released her agenda. Rather than berating herself for not being able to function as she always had, she relaxed. She played simple computer games—the activity kept her hands busy and engaged a small part of her brain in the thinking process again. She stopped lamenting over the things she couldn't do with her children, ages 10, 12, and 13, and began enjoying the things she *could* do, like playing with them on the beach. Gradually the malaise lifted. Her strength and positive outlook returned, and with it came an increased desire for total abandonment to Christ.

Sometimes, like Amy, we experience seasons of life that baffle us. As far as we know, we're not harboring sin in our hearts. We believe our spiritual life is in order, but when we cry out to God, we hear only silence. How should we respond?

We have a choice: wrestle or nestle. We can fret and demand answers. We can work harder for God. Or we can cease striving and trust God to do what's necessary in our lives to burn away the dross. Sometimes He works in ways that hurt, but He always does so to encourage spiritual growth. He loves us so much that He wants us to enjoy His friendship, to pant after Him like a parched deer pants for cool water (Psalm 42:1).

When everything in which we trust is stripped away, we're left with what matters most—our relationship with Jesus Christ. Will we wrestle with Him or nestle in Him?

Inward Glimpse

Dear Father, thank You for inviting me to nestle in You. Help me learn what that means on a daily basis. Amen.

- Write a description of what it means to nestle in God.
- On a scale of one to ten, with ten being the greatest, rate your ability to nestle in God.

Outward Glance

Father, I pray that _____ will find her strength in quietness and trust (Isaiah 30:15). When she comes to crossroads in her life, may she ask for the ancient paths. May she walk in the good way and find rest for her soul (Jeremiah 6:16). Amen.

One More Peek

Be still, and know that I am God;
  I will be exalted among the nations,
  I will be exalted in the earth (Psalm 46:10).

Cave Dwellers

*After the fire came a gentle whisper. When Elijah heard it, he pulled his
cloak over his face and went out and stood at the mouth of the cave.
Then a voice said to him, "What are you doing here, Elijah?"*

1 KINGS 19:12-13

Upward Gaze

My eyes are fixed on you, Sovereign Lord. In You I take
refuge (Psalm 141:8). You are faithful and righteous and
able to come to my relief (Psalm 143:11). Thank You for
being all I need in times of trouble. Amen.

~

Caves aren't the prettiest places to hang out. Cold. Dank. Dark. If
I had to choose a temporary dwelling place, I guarantee it wouldn't be
a hole in a rock. I'd settle for the sandy South Pacific and sip fresh
pineapple juice from sunrise to sunset.

I recently spent several months in a cave. Not a physical one, thank
heavens. It was a spiritual and emotional cave. And believe me, it
wasn't my idea of a good time. Despite the discomfort, however, I
learned that cave dwelling offers some amazing perks.

Remember the story about our car's transmission dying on the day my daughter and I left home for college? The repair bill totaled about $3500. Well, the story didn't end there...

During Stephanie's senior year of high school, Gene and I prayed regularly that the Lord would provide for her upcoming college education. Living on a missionary's salary doesn't leave much for big bills, so we couldn't offer significant financial assistance. When college acceptance handed us a $10,000 expense, our faith felt feeble. We knelt to keep our knees from knocking and bolstered each other with Scripture promises. The transmission's death, however, took our faith-test to a whole new level. Now we were looking at $13,500, and we moved into the cave of fear and discouragement.

The morning after the transmission incident, I felt angry at God for allowing this additional cost. There I was, brushing my teeth (with a little too much force, perhaps?), when suddenly a chunk of one molar flew from my mouth. I'd lost a piece of the same tooth many months prior, but because I'd had no pain, I'd avoided the dentist. Now, minus half a tooth, I needed dental work and a crown. The bill? About $700.

Two days later, we retrieved our car from the repair shop. "It needs a wheel alignment now," said the mechanic.

"Just watch," I said to Gene. "We probably need new tires too." I was right. Another $500. And so it went. Within six weeks, we'd incurred nearly $6000 in expenses above the college tuition.

Gene and I compared our bank account to our expenses and pondered leaving the ministry. *Has God forgotten about our needs? Perhaps it's time to move on.* Remaining at the camp seemed an impossibility, but we knew we couldn't leave without God's go-ahead.

In desperation, we set aside a day to fast and pray. And God answered through Kay Arthur's booklet *The Sovereignty of God*:

> Do you sometimes even wonder if there is a God who cares, who loves, who sees, who knows what is going on in your life? At times does it all seem so frustrating, so futile that you just want to run away?... Where are you? He knows. He sees. Your God is omniscient, all-knowing. You don't have to run away. Stay. He will meet you where you are.[12]

We asked. God answered: "Stay in the cave. I'll meet you there." And He did.

Month by month, He taught us to be content. He reminded us of His presence. He granted faith to believe that He would provide. He even prompted someone to write a check for $500—enough to pay for the tires! And through scholarships, donations, and unexpected student employment, He provided Stephanie's full tuition.

John Ortberg writes,

> Sometimes you are in a cave, and no human action is able to get you out. There is something you can't fix, can't heal, or can't escape, and all you can do is trust God. Finding ultimate refuge in God means you become so immersed in his presence, so convinced of his goodness, so devoted to his lordship that you find even the cave is a perfectly safe place to be because he is there with you.[13]

Sooner or later we all experience cave dwelling. Sometimes it happens when we make a poor choice or when we're stripped of all our props. Sometimes it happens when, try as we might, we simply can't attain a goal we've set for ourselves.

As I said, cave dwelling isn't something I'd choose. It's not my idea of a good time. But it's a rich time. Why? Because God meets us there. As Ortberg says: "God does some of His best work in caves. The cave is where God resurrects dead things."

Inward Glimpse

Dear Father, thank You for meeting me in the cave. Help me be content to stay there. Amen.

- What can you learn about yourself and about God when you're in a cave?
- Jesus spent three days in a cave, and that's when God did His best work ever! How does Christ's resurrection and departure from the cave give you hope?

Outward Glance

Lord, thank You for being _____'s God. Teach her to do
Your will. May Your Holy Spirit lead her on level ground.
Rescue her from her enemies because she hides herself in
You (Psalm 143:8-10). Amen.

One More Peek

I cry to you, O LORD;
  I say, "You are my refuge,
  my portion in the land of the living" (Psalm 142:5).

Choose Praise

I will give thanks to the Lord because of his righteousness
and will sing praise to the name of the Lord Most High.

Psalm 7:17

Upward Gaze

God, I will proclaim Your name and praise Your greatness.
You are the rock; Your works are perfect, and all Your ways
are just. You are a faithful God who does no wrong. You are
upright and just (Deuteronomy 32:3-4). Amen.

~

When my husband and I need a break, we hop on our 27-foot boat
and sail or motor 45 minutes across the Inside Passage to Vancouver
Island. We dock at a marina and walk to a nearby fast-food restaurant
that serves soft ice cream. Recently we invited four friends to join us.

There wasn't a whisper of wind that evening. Gene revved the 9.9
horsepower motor, and we set off, bucking the incoming tide. All went
well for the first half hour. Only 15 minutes from our destination, however, the motor sputtered and died. Gene fiddled with a few switches

200

and pulled the starter cord. The engine started again, but it didn't run for long. It coughed once or twice and then fell silent. One of our friends, a mechanic, took his turn. The same thing happened.

With no propulsion, the boat didn't stand a chance against the tide. The current immediately began carrying our boat up the passage, the opposite direction from the restaurant and its soft ice cream.

Gene worked on the motor until sweat covered his forehead, but it was no use. Six souls stranded on a boat, headed for certain shipwreck... the musical theme for the old television show *Gilligan's Island* began running through my mind.

Have you heard of the story-game "good news, bad news"? If so, you can guess how our situation progressed. The bad news was that our sailboat drifted into the shipping lane where the Alaskan cruise ships and cargo ships travel. The good news was that there were no cruise ships that evening, and the only tugboat and barge visible didn't ram us.

The bad news was that darkness started falling. The good news was that the sunset looked like God Himself had splashed oranges and pinks across the sky.

The bad news was that we were too far from shore to holler for help. The good news was that the Coast Guard picked up our radio distress call.

And so continued our plight. At Gene's request, the Coast Guard phoned our next-door neighbor, who happened to be away from his house at that moment. When he finally got our message, he jumped into a speedboat and rushed to our rescue. He hadn't towed us for long before his boat ran out of gas. Luckily, he'd planned ahead and brought an extra supply. Unfortunately, the boat used that too. But that was okay because our sailboat had an extra tank aboard.

I was raised on the Alberta prairies. The nearest body of water, other than the bathtub and the community pool, was a weedy man-made lake ten miles south of town. Needless to say, I had no association with water, especially rushing tides and giant whirlpools and heavens-knows-what swimming in its dark depths. So when the motor died and refused to be revived, my heart skipped a few beats. When our rescuer ran out of gas, it skipped a few more.

My less-than-ideal circumstances presented me with a choice. I could focus either on the bad news or on the good news. I could fret, or I could pray and praise.

The Bible story about Paul and Silas encouraged me to do the latter. They were stripped, flogged, and thrown into prison with their feet fastened in stocks. Compared to their circumstances, mine looked like a birthday party. How did they respond? They held a songfest! Scripture says, "About midnight Paul and Silas were praying and singing hymns to God" (Acts 16:22-25). If they could praise in those conditions, I could do the same in mine.

Praising God isn't a suggested activity that we might consider when we feel like doing it. Rather, it's a command to be obeyed even when we're not up to it. God knows what He's talking about. He always has a good reason for telling us to do something. And He always enables us to do what He says.

When less-than-ideal situations face us, we can remember Paul and Silas' response and follow their example. Praise—acknowledging God's mighty character—is powerful stuff. It might not change our circumstances, but it honors God. It reminds us that He's in charge, and that knowledge is enough to carry us through whatever we face.

Inward Glimpse

Dear Father, thank You for showing me the power of praise. Help me respond to adverse circumstances as Paul and Silas did. Amen.

- What is your greatest worry? Write a prayer, praising God that He is bigger than that concern and able to work it out for His glory.
- Read the hymn "Jesus! What a Friend for Sinners." From the lyrics, list at least five reasons for praising Jesus.

Outward Glance

God, I pray that _____ will praise You at all times (Psalm 34:1). May her hymns of praise cause many to see and fear and put their trust in You (Psalm 40:3). Amen.

One More Peek

I will praise you, O LORD, with all my heart;
  I will tell of all your wonders.
I will be glad and rejoice in you;
  I will sing praise to your name, O Most High
  (Psalm 9:1-2).

Jesus! What a Friend for Sinners

J. Wilbur Chapman

Jesus! What a Friend for sinners!
Jesus! Lover of my soul;
Friends may fail me, foes assail me,
He, my Saviour, makes me whole.

Jesus! What a Strength in weakness!
Let me hide myself in Him;
Tempted, tried, and sometimes failing,
He, my Strength, my vict'ry wins.

Jesus! What a Help in sorrow!
While the billows o'er me roll,
Even when my heart is breaking,
He, my Comfort, helps my soul.

Jesus! What a Guide and Keeper!
While the tempest still is high,
Storms about me, night o'ertakes me,
He, my Pilot, hears my cry.

Jesus! I do now receive Him,
More than all in Him I find.
He hath granted me forgiveness,
I am His, and He is mine.

Hallelujah! what a Saviour!
Hallelujah! what a Friend!
Saving, helping, keeping, loving,
He is with me to the end.

Play-Doh People

Upward Gaze

Heavenly Father, You're worthy of praise, for You are the perfect Potter. I'm clay in Your hands. I trust You to form my life into the pot of Your choosing, shaping me as seems best to You (Jeremiah 18:1-6). Amen.

~

Housebound by rain for the fifth consecutive day, my kids and several day care children felt crawly. They finger painted, read books, played games, watched videos, and baked cookies, but they needed something different. An activity book suggested homemade Play-Doh. "What do you think, kids?" I asked.

"Yeah!" they cheered.

I mixed, cooked, added food coloring, and kneaded. Within minutes I'd produced a green glob and a blue blob.

After the dough cooled, the kids claimed their portions and set to work using various kitchen tools—a rolling pin, a garlic press, cookie cutters, and toothpicks. They made caterpillars, alphabet letters, eyeglasses, snowmen, and flowers. They finished their projects and then smooshed them and made more.

One girl sat quietly absorbed in her work. "What are you making?" I asked.

"A lady," she said. She rolled four pieces for arms and legs and attached them to the body with toothpicks. She rolled teeny strips for hair and tiny balls for eyes. Finally she leaned back in her chair and surveyed her creation from different angles. She added a nose and announced, "I'm finished. She's perfect. May I take her home?"

"Of course," I said. I tried placing the lady in a box without breaking her, but it was nearly impossible. The slightest movement threatened to break her flimsy body.

A day or so later, a friend told me about a store-bought craft clay. "Heat hardens the clay and makes it strong," she said. "The kids' projects won't break as easily. Try it." I followed her suggestion.

Once again the sculptress set to work. When she finished her project—another little lady—we put it in the oven for a slow bake. After the timer buzzed, we set the lady on the kitchen counter to cool.

"This time she won't break," I said. "The heat made her strong." The girl nodded and smiled.

I smiled too, for the incident reminded me of God's working in our lives. He creates us and pays close attention to every detail. He delights in His workmanship, just as the girl took pride in hers.

Often God uses the heat of disappointment or hardship to strengthen our flimsy faith. When the temperature rises, we might feel like jumping off the pan and running away, but we can remember that God shapes and builds us. He wants us to learn to trust Him even when we don't understand our circumstances. He wants to cleanse our lives from impurities such as impatience, worry, a sharp tongue, or selfishness. He knows what He's doing. He never allows more heat than we can bear.

Our difficult experiences are never in vain. Often they make us more sensitive to others who are "in the oven." We can lend practical help by watching another woman's children when she faces an emergency, providing meals or baked goods for a family in crisis, or donating finances or clothing to those less fortunate. Sometimes we simply need to lend a listening ear or a sympathetic shoulder.

Whatever circumstances we face, we can find encouragement in knowing that we're precious to our Creator. Yes, He'll allow heat in our lives, but it's for a good reason—to strengthen us so He might accomplish His purposes through us.

Inward Glimpse

Father, thank You for strengthening me through heat. When the temperature rises, help me remember that the final outcome is worth it! Amen.

- In what ways has God used heat to make you strong?
- Write a prayer committing to rejoicing in difficulties.

Outward Glance

Father, I pray that _____ will consider it pure joy when she faces various trials. Help her understand that the testing of her faith develops perseverance, and through it she will mature and be complete, lacking nothing (James 1:2-4). Amen.

One More Peek

But he knows the way that I take;
  when he has tested me, I will come forth as gold
  (Job 23:10).

Trustworthy

Surely God is my salvation;
I will trust and not be afraid.
The LORD, the LORD, is my strength and my song;
he has become my salvation.

ISAIAH 12:2

Upward Gaze

Father, You are righteous and save the upright in heart. You are my shield, the one who makes the righteous secure (Psalm 7:9-10). Thank You for promising to provide refuge in the shadow of Your wings. Thank You for sending Your love and faithfulness (Psalm 57:1,3). When I am afraid, I will trust in you (Psalm 56:3). Amen.

~

Betty jumped from her car, ran into her house, and threw some clothes into a suitcase. She glanced at her watch as she recalled the nurse's words: "We're airlifting your husband to a better-equipped hospital. Go home and pack your bags. Return immediately if you hope to fly with him." She grabbed her suitcase and dashed back to the car. Every minute counted.

How could a person's life change so suddenly? Betty wondered. Less than 48 hours earlier, everything was fine. And then the heart attack hit. She remembered waking up when her 52-year-old husband, David, rolled from bed and hit the floor with a thud. She recalled crying Jesus' name aloud, phoning 911, watching the flashing red lights disappear into the darkness, and sitting in the hospital's emergency room. Now this. *What does our future hold? Will David live or die? How will our kids cope in my absence?*

Betty spent the next week at David's bedside in the cardiac critical care unit. Too preoccupied to read her Bible or pray, she felt buoyed by the prayers of family and friends. During this time, a Scripture verse came to her mind over and over: "Surely God is my salvation: I will trust and not be afraid. The LORD, the LORD, is my strength and my song; he has become my salvation" (Isaiah 12:2).

Indeed, God had given her every reason to trust and not be afraid. He'd arranged for David's care at this cardiac unit. He'd provided accommodation and a vehicle for her in the city. He'd provided child care for their kids. He'd even planted Isaiah 12:2 in her thoughts daily for nearly three weeks prior to the heart attack. But what if He took David? The question haunted her. Could she still trust Him if He took her husband?

Day after day, David's condition hovered between life and death. Doctors made treatment plans and then canceled them and debated other options. Uncertainty became a way of life. One afternoon as Betty walked the hospital hallway, she chose to trust completely, regardless of the situation's outcome.

Lord, I don't want my husband to die, she prayed. *He's my best friend. I need him. I have young children. But, Lord, I trust You. If You need his death to fulfill some purpose that's greater than I can see, he's Yours.*

Because of God's position and promises, Betty could trust Him and not be afraid. She surrendered her husband and placed her family's future in the Lord's hands just as Abraham offered Isaac in complete surrender to a God he could not see.

In her book *Surrender: The Heart God Controls*, Nancy Leigh DeMoss refers to Abraham's example:

> Abraham surrendered himself to the purposes and plans of God, with no tangible guarantee that his obedience would ever "pay off." Even when he could not see the outcome of his faith, he *believed* God. He staked his life, his security, his future—everything—on the fact that God was real and that He would keep His promises (Hebrews 11:6). That was the foundation on which his faith rested. That was what motivated his repeated acts of surrender.[14]

We sing songs and hear sermons about trusting God. We read Scriptures that command us to trust and not be afraid. Talking about it is one thing; practicing it is another thing altogether, especially when it hurts. But like Abraham and like Betty, we can choose to believe that God is who He says He is, and we can act upon that truth.

Regardless of the circumstances we face, we can place our trust in this God who has become our salvation. We can choose to praise Him for being our strength and our song. Sometimes doing so requires an act of our will, but that's okay. The result is worth it. We can face fear with courage, and our relationship with Him grows more intimate.

Inward Glimpse

Dear Father, thank You for being trustworthy. When I feel afraid or anxious, remind me of Your faithfulness. Amen.

- Write today's key verse on a 3 x 5 card and memorize it.
- In what situations is God asking you to trust Him?

Outward Glance

Father, I pray that _____ will find her strength in You. May she take refuge in You, her rock. Be her shield, her fortress, and her deliverer. Be her salvation and her stronghold. Save

her from her enemies when she calls to You. And teach her
that You alone are worthy of praise (Psalm 18:1-3). Amen.

One More Peek

Those who know your name will trust in you,
  for you, LORD, have never forsaken those who seek you
  (Psalm 9:10).

A Thankful Heart

Do not be anxious about anything, but in everything, by prayer and petition, with thanksgiving, present your requests to God.

Philippians 4:6

Upward Gaze

I sing for joy to You, Lord. I shout aloud to You, the rock of my salvation. I come before You with thanksgiving and extol You with music and song. You are a great God, the King above all gods (Psalm 95:1-3). Amen.

~

Gene and I moved to Nepal as newlyweds. After five months of informal language study in Kathmandu, we packed a few belongings in rat-proof metal suitcases, boarded a rickety bus, and headed for the hills. Literally. Gene was assigned to work on a hydroelectric power project. I would teach basic health care in our Hindu village and prepare for our first child's birth.

A two-story mud-and-rock dwelling with a thatched roof became our home. It measured three giant steps from front to back and six giant steps from side to side. It had no running water, no electricity, and no indoor plumbing.

First-time experiences kept life interesting for the first few weeks. I hired a teenage girl to help with housework and began teaching her the Nepalese alphabet. I learned to bathe in a plastic basin plopped in the middle of my cow-dung kitchen floor. I learned to cook on a kerosene camping stove and bake using a tiny tin oven. Not bad for a woman who'd never camped!

Three or four months later, however, the monsoon season arrived. Laundry took several days to dry. Termites ate my cookbook. Ants invaded the sugar container. Scorpions sneaked into my house. Vines grew through the walls.

The novelty wore off. I focused on the annoyances and inconveniences, and I turned into a complaint queen.

"I wish the neighbors would stop staring through the windows."

"I'm tired of boiling and filtering water. That's all I do every day—boil and filter."

"The flour is crawling with worms. I have to sift every spoonful before baking cookies. Yuck."

At some point, I think God decided He'd heard enough. He launched a lesson in thanksgiving, filled with real-life visual aids to help me understand its importance. One night, as Gene and I made our pre-bedtime trek to the outhouse, we noticed an orange glow lighting the sky across the valley. The next morning, neighbors told us that a fire had destroyed a family's home and shop. They'd had precious few belongings before the fire. Now they had none.

Shortly after that, I saw a man carry a sick woman in a basket on his back. In the absence of roads and vehicles, he'd backpacked her along steep, winding footpaths for nearly four days in search of medical care.

Then a schoolgirl, perhaps eight years old, stopped by our house. "My mom died last night," she said. "A snake bit her while she slept."

After that, a woman knocked on my door and asked if I had medicine for her sick toddler. She'd already lost four of her eight children and was afraid he would die too.

The visual aids grabbed my attention. When I began looking beyond my trivial troubles and seeing other people's pain, I realized that my griping grieved God. My life brimmed with reasons for thanksgiving, and He wanted to hear about those.

Someone once said, "Happiness comes when we stop wailing about the troubles we have and offer thanks for all the troubles we don't have." That's a life-changing observation, one that presents a great challenge. How can we respond?

Rather than whine about rainy weather, we can give thanks for the moisture and pray for those starving in drought-stricken lands. Rather than complain about walking when we'd rather ride, we can remember people suffering from crippling diseases and thank God for two strong legs. Rather than grumble about losing electrical power in a storm, we can be grateful for modern conveniences and pray for people in third world countries who chop and haul firewood every day so they can cook their food and heat their homes…if they have food and homes, that is.

I've also learned that God's unchanging love and faithfulness give reason for thanksgiving no matter what. Even when we face less than ideal circumstances, God's character never changes. His promises never fail. He's always in control. And He's coming back someday!

How about you? Maybe thanksgiving comes naturally. If so, I'm thrilled for you! If not, think about the troubles you have and purpose to stop wailing about them. Instead, offer thanks for the troubles you don't have. When you do, you'll discover a whole new perspective!

Inward Glimpse

Dear Father, thank You for revealing Your will for my attitude. Help me give thanks in everything. Amen.

- List ten things for which you're thankful.
- List one thing for which you haven't been thankful. Now write a prayer of thanksgiving for it!

Outward Glance

Father, I pray that _____ will give thanks to You because of Your righteousness. Open her mouth to sing praise to Your name (Psalm 7:17). And teach her to give thanks in all circumstances, thereby obeying Your will for her in Christ Jesus (1 Thessalonians 5:18). Amen.

One More Peek

I will praise God's name in song
and glorify him with thanksgiving.
This will please the LORD more than an ox,
more than a bull with its horns and hoofs
(Psalm 69:30-31).

Cross-Stitched Perfection

Many, O Lord my God,
are the wonders you have done.
The things you planned for us
no one can recount to you;
were I to speak and tell of them,
they would be too many to declare.

PSALM 40:5

Upward Gaze

I praise You, Father, for You are the King who reigns wisely. You do what is just and right (Jeremiah 23:5). Your thoughts toward me are precious. If I were to count them, they would outnumber the sand on the seashore (Psalm 139:17-18). Amen.

~

When Stephanie emptied her desk drawers, she discovered an unopened cross-stitch kit. She read the instructions, planted herself on the couch, and began working on the picture—a cartoon version of

Noah's ark stuffed with giraffes, elephants, and other jungle critters. Several weeks later she framed it and gave it to me for my birthday. Next, she stitched a wild-eyed orange cat suspended upside-down from a hanging plant. Then came a lighthouse, followed by a saxophone surrounded by floral bouquets. For nearly seven months, Stephanie spent every free minute working diligently, producing gifts for others to enjoy. Her enthusiasm spread.

After selecting a pattern book containing seaside themes, I began a project of my own—a lighthouse mural. Stitch upon stitch, a palette of colored thread—brick red, turquoise blue, sea-foam green—began transforming blank Aida cloth into a work of art.

Before long, however, my enthusiasm soon waned. For the most part, I found cross-stitching therapeutic after a busy day, but I felt impatient when the thread tangled or knotted. *Oh, no.* Jerk, yank, snip. *This is supposed to be relaxing.* Sometimes the work felt tedious. *In two hours I've stitched one square inch. Will I ever finish this?* If I miscounted stitches and placed one incorrectly, I'd have to remove the stray and try again. Progress dragged. Before long, other projects beckoned, and the lighthouse mural slipped to the bottom of my priority list.

When I consider God as the Master Crafter of our lives, I'm thankful He functions more like Stephanie than like me! He works quietly. Deliberately. Unceasingly. He wants our lives to reflect the beauty of Jesus Christ. He knows this will take time. And He won't quit until it's accomplished.

Sometimes progress slows. A selfish attitude forms a knot in our relationships. An ungrateful heart, like a tangled thread, hinders His work. Anger, a critical spirit, or a wrong motive, like misplaced stitches, must be removed. Setbacks happen, but He never casts us aside to pursue more promising projects. We're always His first priority.

Sometimes the process wearies or frustrates us. We're tempted to speed things up, to turn the Master Crafter's efforts into a do-it-yourself project. Or we ask Him to work in our loved ones' lives, and when we don't see answers as quickly as we'd like, we assume He needs our creative assistance. Our motives may be right, but in our haste, we plant a stitch in the wrong place. We jab the needle or jerk the thread. We snip too soon.

When we grow impatient at the lack of progress in our lives or in the lives of our loved ones, we can remember that God isn't finished yet! He knows what the picture will look like. He'll persevere until He completes it. And when He's finished, He'll present us as His perfect works of art!

Inward Glimpse

Dear Father, thank You for faithfully working in my life and in those I love. Help me trust You and be patient in the process. Amen.

- Write a sentence prayer, giving thanks to God for patiently and unceasingly working in your life.
- What picture do you envision for your life? Your spouse's life? Your children's lives? Write your thoughts and commit them to the Master Crafter.

Outward Glance

Heavenly Father, thank You that Your plans for _____ are good. Make her glad by Your deeds. May she sing for joy at the works of Your hands (Psalm 92:4). May she believe that her times are in Your hands and trust You as her God (Psalm 31:14-15). And may she be strong and take courage as she hopes in You (Psalm 31:24). Amen.

One More Peek

...being confident of this, that he who began a good work in you will carry it on to completion until the day of Christ Jesus (Philippians 1:6).

Beyond My Comfort Zone

Have I not commanded you? Be strong and courageous. Do not be
terrified; do not be discouraged, for the LORD your God
will be with you wherever you go.

JOSHUA 1:9

Upward Gaze

Father, I praise You because You are ever present. You've promised to go ahead of me; You've promised to be with me. You will not fail nor forsake me. And that knowledge guards me from fear (Deuteronomy 31:8). Amen.

≈

Have you ever been stretched w-a-a-a-y beyond your comfort zone? Have you ever felt the knee-knockin' fear that sometimes accompanies new opportunities? If so, you'll understand how I felt recently...

I was living every writer's dream. Starting my first media tour to publicize my first book, *10-Minute Time Outs for Moms*. But there was one little problem: I'd left the security of my island home in British Columbia and landed in unfamiliar and very intimidating territory—

Chicago. To some readers, that's no big deal. But let me explain my background.

My island's population hovers around 4000. The speed limit is 30 miles per hour. We have one gas station and no traffic lights. Drivers must be careful not to hit deer and frogs. Yes, the local newspaper once warned motorists to respect the frogs crossing the highway. And I'm severely directionally challenged; I can lose my way leaving a cul-de-sac. Get the picture?

So there I was, huddled in the airport shuttle, watching cars, buses, and trucks of every size and description zip and zoom along the freeway. Signs pointed north, south, east, and west. Exits left the road in every direction.

Less than an hour after landing at O'Hare, a clerk at a rental agency handed me a set of keys and pointed toward a grey car in the parking lot. "You're all set," he said. "Have a good trip." I almost choked.

I loaded my suitcases into the trunk and reread the directions my publicist had sent me. *Maybe I should review these instructions with the clerk,* I thought. *One can never be too careful!* I retraced my steps. The clerk glanced at the directions and said, "Don't follow these! I know a shortcut."

With an authority that surprised even me, I said, "No, thank you! If I take a shortcut, you'll see my face on a milk carton in a few weeks!" He stared at me as though I'd lost my mind. "I live on a remote island! I'm directionally challenged! If I take one wrong exit, I'm doomed. Poof! Gone forever." He laughed and complied with my request.

Moments later, I was sitting in the driver's seat of my rental car. The clerk had laughed, but I didn't see the humor. I was a galaxy beyond my comfort zone. My heart threatened to pound out of my chest. And then it happened—God spoke.

Gently but firmly, the words of Joshua 1:9 came to mind: "Have I not commanded you? Be strong and courageous. Do not be terrified; do not be discouraged, for the LORD your God will be with you wherever you go."

I knew the words were true. Then and there I made a deliberate choice to believe, and I whispered a prayer: *I will not let fear control me. God, You've brought me this far, and You won't abandon me now.* I patted the passenger seat beside me. *Okay, God. It's You and me. Open my eyes to see the right exits. Put a shield around my car. Thank You for being with me now.*

My heart rate slowed. My blood pressure lowered. An undeniable peace settled over me as I meditated on Joshua 1:9. And I navigated unfamiliar territory without incident.

I'll cherish the memory forever. Why? Because God stretched me far beyond my comfort zone, and as a result, I discovered a greater appreciation for, and understanding of, His promised presence.

When God plunks us into situations beyond our comfort zone, our first reaction is often fear. The unknowns unnerve us. But God understands our emotions, so He reminds us of His presence. We can either allow fear to control us or we can recognize it as an opportunity to experience His presence in a new way.

New opportunities can sometimes be frightening, but we're never alone. *Never.* God's presence goes with us wherever our journey leads, even into unfamiliar territory.

Inward Glimpse

Heavenly Father, thank You for not sending me into unfamiliar territory alone. You're with me everywhere I go. Amen.

- Recall a situation which plunked you outside your comfort zone. How did you respond? How did this experience teach you more about God's character?

- Read the lyrics from the hymn "How Gentle God's Commands." How do the words apply to us when we're outside our comfort zone?

Outward Glance

Father, when You lead _____ into new opportunities that stretch her beyond her comfort zone, please keep her from feeling fainthearted. Guard her from fear. Remind her that You are the Lord and that You are with her. Reassure her that You will fight against her enemies to save her (Deuteronomy 20:3-4). Amen.

One More Peek

When you pass through the waters,
   I will be with you;
and when you pass through the rivers,
   they will not sweep over you (Isaiah 43:2).

How Gentle God's Commands

Phillip Doddridge

How gentle God's commands!
How kind His precepts are!
Come, cast your burdens on the Lord,
And trust His constant care.

Beneath His watchful eye
His saints securely dwell;
That hand which bears all nature up
Shall guard His children well.

Why should this anxious load
Press down your weary mind?
Haste to your heavenly Father's throne,
And sweet refreshment find.

His goodness stands approved,
Unchanged from day to day:
I'll drop my burden at His feet
And bear a song away.

Masks

But if we walk in the light, as he is in the light,
we have fellowship with one another, and the blood of Jesus,
his Son, purifies us from all sin. If we claim to be
without sin, we deceive ourselves and the truth is not in us.

1 JOHN 1:7-8

Upward Gaze

God, You have searched me and known me. You know everything I do, and You know my thoughts from afar. Nothing is hidden from You (Psalm 139:1-2). I praise You for being an all-knowing God, one from whom I cannot hide anything. Amen.

~

Beginning in early October, many stores sell Halloween masks. Some wear friendly smiles, like television's Miss Piggy or the purple dinosaur, Barney. Others, made to resemble Count Dracula or witches with nose warts, don't look as innocent.

Cultures worldwide embrace the tradition of wearing masks, or false faces, for various festivals and rituals. Some construct them from paper or plastic. Others use wood, shells, leather, or metal. Some simply paint the face with colorful patterns. Regardless of their design or material, they serve one purpose—to hide the wearer's physical identity.

The same purpose holds true for emotional masks—women sometimes don a false face to conceal their true identity from others. For example, a stressed-out mother hollers at her kids through Sunday morning breakfast and then walks into church with a pasted-on smile lest someone thinks she's unspiritual. A woman struggling with post-abortive memories hides behind jokes and laughter lest others detect her sorrow. Or a woman shrouds herself in silence lest someone discovers her abusive history.

Cheryl wore the mask of silence. She divorced her husband many years before she became a Christian. He retaliated by kidnapping their only child and moving across the country. When Cheryl finally located them, he agreed to let her see the boy for two weeks each year. Distance made those visits difficult. As the boy grew older, they became less frequent and eventually stopped altogether.

Cheryl regretted the situation. She carried pain and guilt until she placed her saving faith in Jesus Christ and received His forgiveness. But for the next 15 years, she remained silent whenever conversation with friends centered on their children. *They'll reject me if they discover that I didn't raise my son,* she reasoned. She shared her history only when she felt safe with select individuals.

During this time, Cheryl relocated and began attending a new church. Several months later, she started a weekly book club and invited women from the congregation. As they read *The Purpose-Driven Life,* they discussed the path to meaningful relationships—removing emotional masks, letting one's guard down, dispensing with polite but shallow conversation. They also discovered truths about fellowship:

> In real fellowship people experience authenticity. It happens when people get honest about who they are and what is happening in their lives. They share their hurts, reveal their feelings,

confess their failures, disclose their doubts, admit their fears, acknowledge their weaknesses, and ask for help and prayer.[15]

The words convicted Cheryl about her lack of transparency with the women. *I need to lower my mask and tell people who I really am*, she thought. *I need to tell others how God has freed me from the pain I've suffered.* She swallowed her fear, risked rejection, and spilled her story, focusing on God's forgiveness and the freedom He'd granted. Doing so gave her an even greater sense of freedom—she no longer had to worry about what others would think about her if they discovered her secret. And her honesty moved the group from polite chitchat to authenticity where meaningful relationships could grow.

Hiding behind masks can be so easy. We want others to believe we're perfect and problem free. We want them to think we're strong and capable of handling life, come what may. Heaven forbid they discover we're worried about our kids' friendships, or struggling in our marriage, or battling bulimia.

But when we remove our masks and allow others to see our true identity, others feel safe and remove theirs too. When honesty prevails, we can pray for one another's struggles, celebrate the victories, and press on toward maturity.

Inward Glimpse

Father, thank You for encouraging me to remove the masks. Help me be honest with others, and may they be honest with me, so we can encourage one another along the journey. Amen.

- Are you wearing a mask to conceal your history or a particular struggle? If so, what will you do about it?

- If you sense that another woman is hiding behind a mask, pray for her today. Send her a note of encouragement.

Outward Glance

Father, I pray that _____ will encourage others in their faith, and that by doing so, she will also experience growth (Romans 1:12). May she make every effort to do what leads to peace and to mutual edification (Romans 14:19). Amen.

One More Peek

Therefore confess your sins to each other and pray for each other so that you may be healed. The prayer of a righteous man is powerful and effective (James 5:16).

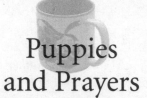

Puppies
and Prayers

I tell you the truth, anyone who will not receive
the kingdom of God like a little child will never enter it.

MARK 10:15

Upward Gaze

Father in heaven, hallowed is Your name. Your kingdom come, Your will be done on earth as it is in heaven (Matthew 6:9-10). You are God over all, yet You invite me into Your presence through prayer and answer my requests. I'm humbled and grateful. Thank You. Amen.

❧

Margaret's knickknack shelf looks different from most. Rather than holding baby pictures and ceramic ornaments, her shelf contains an odd assortment: a tiny china house, a teeny teddy bear, a number "five" candle, a miniature wooden heart, a crèche scene. Each object represents an answered prayer, like a memorial to God's goodness in her family's life. One item, a leather puppy collar, reminds them that God hears the prayers offered in childlike faith.

Throughout her growing up years, Margaret had owned a pet dog. She'd hoped her three children would someday enjoy a dog as well, but when they were old enough to show interest, her husband refused. Margaret compensated by taking them to the local SPCA. There the children learned how to approach dogs and began enjoying their company. Before long, they wanted their own pet.

Margaret wanted to respect her husband's feelings. "Not yet," she replied. "It's not on Papa's agenda, but we can pray about it."

And pray they did. With simple but earnest expressions, the children secretly asked God for a dog. Margaret listened, marveling at their persistent confidence. But she knew her husband's resistance and thought of the odds against their request being answered. *Their faith is stronger than mine,* she thought.

On one SPCA visit, Margaret and her children fell in love with a litter of six puppies—four males and two females. At home that evening, the kids told their dad about the furry, grey dogs. He looked at Margaret and said, "Were they keeshonds? My brother had a keeshond 25 years ago. I haven't seen one since. They're the only dogs I've ever liked."

Margaret and the kids exchanged hopeful glances. She phoned the SPCA. Sure enough, the puppies were purebred keeshonds. Several days later, her husband suggested visiting the kennel but maintained his stance: "No dogs!" His conviction crumbled when he saw the puppies. "I want a female," he said. The family chose the litter's quietest member and arranged to take her home after she was weaned.

God had answered the kids' simple prayers, but only in part. One hurdle remained that no one anticipated.

Margaret and her four-year-old son visited the puppies a week later. Upon seeing the animals, the child said, "Mommy, I don't like our new puppy. I don't want her."

The boy's words surprised Margaret. "Why don't you want her?" she asked.

"Because she's sick."

A veterinarian had examined the puppy and declared her healthy. Why, then, did the child insist the dog was sick? Margaret and her husband couldn't understand, but they obtained permission to exchange her for the only remaining female. Two days later, the first puppy died.

God thoroughly answered the prayers offered in simple faith. The family got their pet. Of all the dogs in the world, she was the only breed and sex Margaret's husband would allow. Pretty good, eh?

I believe God delights in prayers offered in childlike faith. He's our Abba Father. He embodies all the qualities a perfect earthly daddy would possess—self-control, kindness, patience, gentleness, and love. He encourages us to run to Him and pour out our hearts to Him at anytime. And He wants to give us good gifts.

Sometimes we hinder Him from doing so by doubting His abilities. For instance, despite careful stewardship, our monthly expenses outweigh the income. We ask God to provide, but then we worry about how He'll do it.

Or we doubt that He cares about our seemingly insignificant concerns, so we don't tell Him our needs. After all, He's busy operating an entire universe. Why would He care about our child needing athletic shoes or the car needing new tires?

When we talk with God, we can rest assured that He wants to answer our prayers, and He doesn't care if they're polished. He's more interested in our possessing a childlike faith that believes He can and will answer our prayers.

Inward Glimpse

Dear Lord, thank You for honoring childlike faith. Guard me from doubting Your ability or willingness to answer. Amen.

- Write a short prayer praising God for His ability to answer your requests. Thank Him that in His wisdom, He may say no or wait.
- Write today's "One More Peek" verse on a 3 x 5 card and memorize it.

Outward Glance

Father, I pray that _____ will have faith in You. When she tells You her requests, give her the faith to believe that she has already received the answer (Mark 11:24). Amen.

One More Peek

So I say to you: Ask and it will be given to you; seek and you will find; knock and the door will be opened to you. For everyone who asks receives; he who seeks finds; and to him who knocks, the door will be opened (Luke 11:9-10).

Just Love Them

The LORD is gracious and righteous;
our God is full of compassion.
The LORD protects the simplehearted;
when I was in great need, he saved me.

PSALM 116:5-6

Upward Gaze

Dear Lord, I praise You because You're the father of compassion and the God of all comfort (2 Corinthians 1:3). When I'm helpless and hopeless, You redeem my life from the pit and crown me with love and compassion (Psalm 103:4,6). I don't deserve Your kindness, but I gratefully accept it. Thank You!

~

Publicly, Penny's life seemed picture perfect. In 1979, she and her husband, Ted, enjoyed successful careers selling real estate and insurance. They shared three beautiful children, a waterfront home, and a boat. Privately, however, Ted struggled with alcoholism.

Penny struggled to keep their marriage intact, but her husband's addiction only escalated. One night, Ted tearfully confessed his involvement in the homosexual community. In 1987, he tested positive for HIV. A year later, he left the family home and filed for divorce.

As Penny and her children struggled through their situation, a friend invited them to attend an inner-city church. There, surrounded by the mentally handicapped, drug addicts, prostitutes, and homosexuals, Penny discovered emotional support and developed compassion for society's outcasts.

While enrolled in a college course about death and dying, Penny interviewed a 41-year-old AIDS patient abandoned by friends and family. Her heart broke as she watched him lose his balance while trying to perform simple tasks. *God,* she cried, *no one should have to die alone.*

You're right, He seemed to say. *What are you going to do about it?*

I don't know, she said. *I'm not a nurse. I don't like being around sick people.*

How do you like to be treated when you're sick? He asked.

I want someone to check on me, to bring me food if I'm hungry, to bring my medicine. I don't want to be hovered over, but I want to know there's someone I can call on when I have a need.

Exactly. Do that for others. Just love them. It's that simple.

Penny obeyed. When her ex-husband developed AIDS and a brain tumor, she quit her job and drove 40 miles daily to take him to radiation treatments. Later, she used donated funds to purchase a 3300-square-foot home to house dying AIDS patients. Against opposition, she and a small band of volunteers provided a loving environment for more than 40 people in five years—mostly men ages 28 to 63. All found peace with God before they died.

More recently, Penny purchased a vacated, 75,000-square-foot hospital and is now raising nearly two million dollars for renovations. Why? To provide housing for 40 AIDS patients at a time and to train young people to love and serve those often considered society's outcasts (see www.ywamkansas.com—New Jerusalem Missions). She's also using her knowledge to help those impacted by the South African AIDS pandemic.

Penny's life beautifully reflects Jesus Christ's earthly ministry. Without condoning sinful behavior, she loves the sinner. Jesus did the same. He mingled with the tax collectors and prostitutes. He touched the untouchables—literally (Mark 1:41). He addressed the physical needs of the lame, the blind, and the sick. Onlookers questioned His motives. Spectators questioned His sanity. But He ignored their skepticism and fulfilled His mission, healing those broken in body and spirit.

How can we, like Penny, reflect Christ's compassion toward those whom society tends to shun, especially when our lives are already so busy? Here are a few ideas: Donate funds to charitable organizations. Give food, clothing, or blankets to homeless shelters. Donate clothing or special personal hygiene items to women's shelters. Share Christmas gifts and summer camping opportunities with prisoners' children through the Angel Tree project (see www.angeltree.org). Adopt a lonely senior in a local nursing home.

The needs are endless. So are creative opportunities to love. Let's ask God to open our eyes to the needs of society's outcasts. And let's make ourselves available to Him. We won't all be led to do what Penny is doing, but we *can* make a difference in people's lives. How?

Just love them. It's that simple.

Inward Glimpse

Dear Father, thank You for modeling compassion through Jesus Christ's example. Open my eyes to see needs. Open my heart to touch lives. Make my heart compassionate like Yours. Amen.

- Mother Teresa once said, "Let's concentrate on a worthwhile goal: that no child be unwanted, that no person go unloved. And let's not stop smiling at whomever we meet, especially when it's hard to smile." Write this quote on a recipe card and post it where you will see it often. Make it a daily prayer and ask God to give you opportunities to practice it.

- List three ways that you can show compassion and practical love to those considered societal outcasts.

Outward Glance

Dear Father, I pray that _____ will clothe herself with compassion, kindness, humility, gentleness, and patience (Colossians 3:12). May she, like You, work righteousness and justice for all the oppressed (Psalm 103:6). Amen.

One More Peek

The King will reply, "I tell you the truth, whatever you did for one of the least of these brothers of mine, you did for me" (Matthew 25:40).

Restoration Specialist

I will repay you for the years the locusts have eaten...
You will have plenty to eat, until you are full,
and you will praise the name of the LORD your God,
who has worked wonders for you;
never again will my people be shamed.

JOEL 2:25-26

Upward Gaze

Father, it's good to sing praises to You, for You build up Jerusalem; You gather the exiles of Israel. You heal the brokenhearted and bind up their wounds. You grant peace to Your people and satisfy them with the finest of wheat (Psalm 147:1-3,14). Amen.

∾

Emotional bumps and bruises plagued Brian and Gloria's first year of married life. Blending their families presented unforeseen challenges. Since Brian's divorce five years prior, his 16-year-old daughter, Marie, had been the household's female head. She played pseudo-mom to her younger sister and grew accustomed to managing the family home as she wished.

Her dad's second marriage changed that. The teen felt displaced. She felt threatened and angry if Gloria so much as moved a picture. Following another woman's standards or being told no infuriated her.

One evening, Marie huddled under a pile of blankets on her bed and verbally vented her frustration. Gloria sat on the edge of the bed and listened quietly. "It wouldn't matter to me if Dad had married a queen," the teen stated matter-of-factly. "I would still hate her."

The words stung, but Gloria empathized. "I understand," she said finally. "Thank you for telling me how you feel." In the following weeks and months, she encouraged Marie's honest communication. She practiced kindness and patience, but nothing bridged the gap.

The tension continued, but one day while reading her Bible, Gloria discovered today's key verse—Joel 2:25-26. *That's it!* she thought. *My relationship with Marie is as barren as a locust-infested grain field. But God can restore it. He can change it from devastation to a bumper crop.*

Gloria began asking God to restore what the locusts of anger and bitterness had devoured. She longed for healing, for a hate-free bond. More than a decade passed before she saw answers, but she refused to stop praying or lose hope.

Marie's heart gradually softened. Years later, when she planned her wedding, she invited Gloria to help her shop for a bridal gown. At the ceremony, she presented Gloria as her mother rather than as her father's wife. She introduced Gloria's grown children as her brothers and sisters. The word "step" was never voiced.

We marvel at God's ability to rebuild fractured relationships, but why does that surprise us? After all, He specializes in restoration. He can bring healing even when a situation appears beyond hope.

Take an unraveling marriage, for example. A Christian woman recently told me that she'd had an affair several years prior and had become pregnant. She ended the affair and confessed her adultery to her husband, and he forgave her. That almost sounds trite, but don't be mistaken. The emotional pain nearly overwhelmed them at times. Nevertheless, when the woman gave birth, her husband loved and honored the baby as he did his own children. Five years later, the couple enjoys a marriage that is being restored daily. Amazing? Absolutely. And humanly impossible apart from the Spirit of God working in people's lives.

God's Spirit restores other relationships as well. Perhaps a long-standing family feud makes reunions or Christmas get-togethers impossible. Maybe a misunderstanding with a coworker or neighbor causes stress. Perhaps zero communication with our teen frustrates and disappointments us. Whatever our scenario, we long for unity and wonder if strife will *ever* be resolved.

In times like this, we can ask the Lord to show us whether or not we're at fault and, if we are, to give us the strength to ask forgiveness or do whatever is necessary to rectify the situation. We can claim His promise to make all things new. And we can praise Him in advance for His ability to transform hearts through His Holy Spirit's power.

We can also trust Him to give us the hope we need to persevere in prayer. Sometimes the answer to our prayers takes years. In fact, we might not see it happen in our lifetime, but that doesn't mean God isn't working. It just means He's working on a different timetable than we do. Persevering is our role; answering our prayers and fulfilling His promises is His.

Inward Glimpse

Dear Father, thank You for being a restoration specialist. Help me trust You to restore what the locusts have eaten and to fill me with good things. Amen.

- How has God restored the years the locusts have eaten in your life or in the life of someone you know?
- Write a short prayer praising God for His ability to restore broken relationships.

Outward Glance

Father, please hear _____ when she cries out to You. Deliver her from all her troubles. When she's brokenhearted, be near to her. Save her when she feels crushed in spirit (Psalm 34:17-18). Thank You! Amen.

One More Peek

How good and pleasant it is
  when brothers live together in unity! (Psalm 133:1).

Wash Judas' Feet

But I tell you who hear me: Love your enemies,
do good to those who hate you, bless those who curse you,
pray for those who mistreat you.

LUKE 6:27-28

Upward Gaze

God, You're perfect in every way. You cause the sun to rise on the evil and the good, and You send rain on the righteous and the unrighteous (Matthew 5:45). Thank You for showing me how to treat friends and enemies alike. Amen.

~

I grew up in the church. Well, not literally. What I mean is, I spent a lot of time there—twice on Sundays and a couple of times during the week. I left home to sit through three years of Bible school classes, after which I became a missionary, a Sunday school teacher, and a retreat speaker. After all the sermons I've heard and all the Bible lessons I've prepared, I'm still discovering life-changing truths in God's Word. Let me give you an example...

For years I'd heard about the Last Supper and how Jesus washed His disciples' feet (John 13:2-17). But I only recently understood that action's significance. You see, when Jesus washed the feet of every person present, He included Judas—His betrayer.

Scripture says that Jesus knew Judas' intentions (Luke 22:21-22). Despite that, He treated His traitor with the same honor He gave the other disciples. Judas would plant the kiss of death on His cheek in a few hours; nevertheless, Jesus held his feet and gently washed the dust away. Humanly speaking, who could do such a thing? It's almost ludicrous.

If I'd been wearing Jesus' sandals, I might not have responded with such grace. I might have squeezed Judas' feet a little too tight and given them a sandpaper scrub. Better yet, I might have bypassed him altogether and seized the opportunity to humiliate him.

Let's capture the essence of the upper room scene in modern-day terms. Thirteen women gather for a weekend retreat. They've spent years building intimate relationships, laughing and crying together, helping each other in practical ways. But two share a dark secret—one had an affair with the other's husband.

On the last evening together, the first woman enters the meeting room carrying 12 beautifully wrapped gifts. One by one she distributes them, shares an encouraging word, and adds a hug. When she comes to her betrayer, she treats her with the same honor she's shown the rest. No one suspects the treachery.

Who can respond with such kindness?

We can—if we follow Jesus' example and ask the Holy Spirit for grace and strength. Most of us have at least one Judas in our lives. Perhaps that person spoke a lie about us. Maybe she swindled us. Perhaps she took the credit we deserved for a job well done. At any rate, this person has wounded or offended us in some way. How can we, figuratively speaking, wash his or her feet? Here are a few ideas.

The moderator of a committee consistently belittles our ideas. We can thank her for her hard work and ask if we can help in any way.

The mother-in-law gives unwelcome advice. Again. We can hug her and tell her that we're thankful for the fantastic job she did raising her son.

The ex-husband makes unkind comments in front of the children. We can address our concern privately and refuse to hurl hurtful words back.

Regardless of the situation, we can pray for our Judas' spiritual well-being. Not that lightning from heaven will strike him or her but that God will bless. We can also ask the Lord to change our hearts and love that person through us. Our Judas may never change, but we can.

Washing our Judas' feet may seem downright impossible. But because the Holy Spirit lives in us, we can do it. Jesus showed us by example. We just have to follow.

Inward Glimpse

Dear Father, thank You for Christ's example. Help me follow it by washing my Judas' feet. Amen.

- Who's the Judas in your life? Name two ways you can wash his or her feet. Ask God to provide the opportunity and strength to do these things.
- God says that we'll be blessed by following Christ's example (John 13:17). With that in mind, record what happens when you wash your Judas' feet.

Outward Glance

Father, I pray that _____ will model Christ. May she love not only those who love her but her enemies as well. May she pray for those who persecute her. In doing so, may she reflect You—her heavenly Father (Matthew 5:43-44,48). Amen.

One More Peek

Do to others as you would have them do to you (Luke 6:31).

The Lord's Delights

How priceless is your unfailing love!
Both high and low among men
find refuge in the shadow of your wings.
They feast on the abundance of your house;
you give them drink from your river of delights.

PSALM 36:7-8

Upward Gaze

God, I praise You for being a Father who gives good gifts to those who ask You (Matthew 7:11). You are able to do immeasurably more than all we ask or imagine, according to Your power that is at work within us (Ephesians 3:20). I love watching You work! Amen.

~

Rhoda, a servant girl, heard the knock first. "Who is it?" she asked before opening the door.

"Peter," a voice replied. "Let me in."

Rhoda's jaw dropped. *Peter? He's in prison! But no, he's here! How is this possible?* Without stopping to open the door, she turned and ran to the room where believers had gathered to pray. "Peter's here!" she shouted.

"No—you're mistaken," an elderly man said.

"He's here, I tell you!"

"It must be his angel."

The crowd agreed that Rhoda had lost her mind, but she persisted. Finally, several believers opened the door together. Sure enough. Rhoda was right.

There stood Peter—the disciple who'd been arrested, thrown into prison, chained, guarded by 16 soldiers, and scheduled for a public trial. His friends had gathered to pray on his behalf, but their request seemed so far beyond reach. If their prayers for his release were to be answered, it would take an act of God. No human hand could do such a thing.

Use your imagination and put yourself in that house for a moment. Can you hear the questions? Can you feel the bear hugs? Can you see the joy on everyone's faces?

Every answer to prayer brings cause for rejoicing, but sometimes God answers so magnificently that we're left awestruck. There's no doubt that God Himself heard and responded. What fun! With sheer delight we revel in watching Him work.

Winnie enjoyed such an experience recently. She and her husband had decided to move, but they were physically exhausted and didn't think they could cope with the pressures of listing and showing their house. One afternoon, she expressed her concerns to God.

"Lord, we believe that moving is the right thing to do, but You know our physical limitations right now. I've heard people talk about selling their houses without their doing anything about it. Would You please do that for us? I don't know how, but I know You can." She paused and then added one more request. "And when the right buyer comes along, please confirm to her that this is her house."

Two weeks later, Winnie received a notice from a real estate agent. It said that a client was interested in that neighborhood and asked if she'd be willing to show her house. She usually disregarded such notices. This time, however, she discussed it with her husband. They invited the agent to view their home, but after doing so, he decided against its suitability.

Five days later, while Winnie's family hosted out-of-town guests, the agent phoned them. "I have a couple here. I think your place would be perfect for them, but they're leaving town tomorrow. May I show them the house today?"

"I've not done anything to prepare," stammered Winnie.

"That's okay," he said.

Winnie quickly vacuumed and then loaded family and friends into a vehicle and drove away. The agent phoned later that day. "Congratulations! It sold!" he said. "By the way, something unusual happened. The minute the couple stepped into the entryway, the wife began crying and said, 'This is my house.' I've been in the real estate business for 17 years, but I've never seen anything like this."

Thankfulness overwhelmed Winnie. Her prayers were answered so completely that she had no doubt God had done it. And with sheer delight, she reveled in watching Him work.

Let's relish such stories, such "God moments" when His presence seems so real. They build our faith. They remind us that God is God and nothing is too difficult for Him. Best of all, they remind us that the God of the universe wants us to enjoy His friendship. He wants us to drink from the river of His delights and to discover the depths of His love.

Perhaps, when we pray, we should seal our requests with these words: "I don't know how You'll answer, but I believe You can do it. Leave me awestruck, Lord."

I'd love to hear His answers to your prayers! (Send me a note using the contact window in my website—www.gracefox.com.)

Inward Glimpse

Dear Father, thank You for the privilege and delight of watching You work. Keep my eyes wide open so I don't miss Your magnificence. Amen.

- Record your prayers and God's answers in a journal. If you have children at home, do the same with a family journal so they become aware of God's faithfulness.

- Describe an instance when you saw God answer prayer so completely that He was obviously at work.

Outward Glance

Father, I pray that _____ will delight herself in You and that You will give her the desires of her heart (Psalm 37:4). May she revel in Your love, which reaches to the heavens, and Your faithfulness, which reaches to the skies (Psalm 36:5). Amen.

One More Peek

Many, O LORD my God,
  are the wonders you have done.
The things you planned for us
  no one can recount to you;
were I to speak and tell of them,
  they would be too many to declare (Psalm 40:5).

Meeting
God's Standard

*And now, O Israel, what does the LORD your God ask of you
but to fear the LORD your God, to walk in all his ways,
to love him, to serve the LORD your God with all your heart and
with all your soul, and to observe the LORD's commands
and decrees that I am giving you today for your own good?*

DEUTERONOMY 10:12-13

Upward Gaze

One thing I ask of You, Lord. This is what I seek: that I may
dwell in Your house and gaze upon Your beauty. My heart
cries out, *Seek His face!* You alone will I seek, for You have
been my helper and my Savior (Psalm 27:4,8-9). Amen.

∾

Years ago, I cleaned house for several women. Besides turning me
into a semi-professional floor scrubber and vacuum queen, the job gave
me an informal education in human psychology.

247

Typically, when I arrived, the houses appeared tidy. Granted, the bathroom fixtures needed polishing, the windows needed wiping, and the garbage cans needed emptying. But for the most part, things looked pretty good. I thought this was the norm, especially for one home in particular. I was wrong.

One morning, I unlocked the front door and stepped inside as usual. But this time, the landscape looked as though the dryer had exploded—*kaboom!* Jeans, T-shirts, stray socks, and underwear littered the living room floor. Sticky dishes filled the kitchen sink and covered the counters. Newspapers hid the couch and recliner chair. Wet towels dripped on the bathroom floor.

What in the world happened here? I wondered, but not for long. I had no time to waste. I rolled up my sleeves and set to work. Four hours later, the house sparkled.

Later that evening, that homeowner phoned me. "I'm so embarrassed!" she said. "The house was a mess! I forgot you were coming, or I would have tidied up. You won't quit working for me, will you?"

"Of course not," I reassured her. "I clean houses, remember? And if you keep tidying up before I come, you'll put me out of work!"

The woman laughed. "Thank you for understanding." She paused for a moment. "You know something? Working full-time outside my home leaves me exhausted. I wish my husband and kids would help clean the house, but frankly, I'm too tired to force the issue.

"My mom's house was always immaculate. For years I nearly put myself in a grave trying to meet her standards, but it was no use. Hiring you has helped. But in all honesty, I've always straightened the house before cleaning day because I was afraid of what you'd think if you saw the way it looks sometimes. Now my secret's out!"

We talked a few minutes more. I told her that when my three children were preschoolers, I felt pressured to meet others' standards too. In fact, before overnight guests came, I cleaned my house until it glistened. I even dismantled and washed the dining room and bedroom light fixtures! After all, I reasoned, what would people think of me if the lights looked dusty? We ended our conversation with a hearty laugh and a new sense of freedom.

We women are a funny breed! We often worry about meeting other people's standards. Sometimes those expectations are real; sometimes they're only perceived. But it makes no difference. We work and work and work, trying to measure up, to meet their approval. We forget that the only approval we need comes from the Lord.

What is the Lord's standard for our lives? It's certainly not that we keep a picture-perfect, eat-off-the-floor home, although He wants us to be wise stewards and good testimonies to those around us. He cares about one thing and states it plainly in Scripture: "He has showed you, O man, what is good. And what does the LORD require of you? To act justly and to love mercy and to walk humbly with your God" (Micah 6:8).

When we live our lives according to God's standards as shown in that verse, we win His approval. And in doing so, we often earn a good reputation in man's sight. Sometimes, however, an individual may criticize everything we do. If that happens, we can remember that if we're walking God's way and pleasing Him with our actions and attitudes, that's all that really matters.

Inward Glimpse

Dear Father, thank You for teaching me Your standards. Help me remember that Your approval is the only one that's important. Amen.

- Have you been living according to man's standards? If so, in what area? What has the result been?
- Ask the Lord to help you live according to His requirements as stated in Micah 6:8. Thank Him that He's placed His Holy Spirit within you to help you succeed.

Outward Glance

Father, I pray that _____ will love You with all her heart and soul and mind and strength. And teach her to love her neighbor as herself, for in doing so, she obeys the greatest commandments of all (Mark 12:30-31). Amen.

One More Peek

The LORD *does not look at the things man looks at. Man looks at the outward appearance, but the* LORD *looks at the heart* (1 Samuel 16:7).

A Greater Good

Let us fix our eyes on Jesus, the author and perfecter of our faith,
who for the joy set before him endured the cross, scorning its shame,
and sat down at the right hand of the throne of God.

HEBREWS 12:2

Upward Gaze

Father, I praise You for the example set by Your Son. Although He existed in the form of God, He made Himself nothing and took on the nature of a servant in human likeness, humbling Himself and becoming obedient to death so that I could have eternal life (Philippians 2:6-8). Thank You for loving me that much. Amen.

~

"You'll have to use your imagination tonight," said a college-aged camp counselor to 45 kids crouched around a fireless pit. "We'd love to have a real fire, but unfortunately they're banned. It's been too hot and dry. One stray spark in the forest could mean big trouble."

"You mean we can't roast hot dogs?" asked a 12-year-old.

"That's right."

"What about s'mores?" asked another. "If we can't roast marsh-mallows, we can't have s'mores."

"Oh yes, we can. We'll eat the marshmallows raw!" said the coun-selor.

"No way! We want 'em sticky!"

And so the discussion went. The kids tried to convince the counselor to strike a match and light the fire, but it was no use. The warden had posted the sign for all to see: "The use of open campfires is prohibited in this area." Obedience was not optional.

The warden's campfire ban affected more than the menu at the kids' camps. It also changed the atmosphere of the teen camp's evening pro-gram. Normally, the fire's soothing snap and crackle filled the gap between testimonies. Now there was only silence. On many occasions after the program ended, a few individuals remained near the flames' warmth as they spoke about parents, school, friendships, and God. But this night, no one stayed behind.

My husband, the camp program director, considered the ban unfortunate. After all, what's camping without a fire? But he under-stood the importance of respecting the warden's authority. Thousands of towering fir trees stood in clusters around the property. A fire could destroy timber and buildings—the horseback riding arena and barns, the dining room and main lodge, A-frame cabins, a guesthouse, staff homes, tents, and many other structures. It could spread across the island, endangering homes, businesses, and the ecotourism industry.

Disappointment was real, but the stakes were high. For the sake of the greater good, staff and campers set aside their own desires until the warden lifted the ban.

Life's like that, isn't it? Circumstances don't always happen the way we wish. Sometimes we have to forego our desires for the sake of the greater good, even if we don't find the process pleasant or convenient.

Women face this on a small scale every day. As mothers, we rarely find time to read a novel or enjoy a relaxing bath. We set aside our desires and show our kids preference by reading bedtime stories, helping them study for midterm exams, or driving them to extracur-riculars.

Perhaps we reach the weekend on a weary note. We'd rather eat out than prepare another meal. But that costs money, and money is scarce because the kids need braces and college tuition. We choose to respect the family budget and thaw a pound of hamburger instead.

Maybe we're packing our bags for a long-overdue vacation when the phone rings—an elderly parent has fallen and injured himself. The doctor wants his recovery supervised. We cancel our holiday and honor Dad by bringing him home until he's healed.

These examples show the principle of setting aside one's own desires for a greater good. But Jesus Christ's example tops our greatest imaginings. Rather than coming to earth and establishing a comfy kingship, He fixed His eyes on something far better—obeying His Father's will to achieve the greater good—victory over death and eternity in heaven for all who believe in Him.

Our campers and summer staff obeyed the fire warden's words for the sake of the greater good—the protection of life on Quadra Island. Did his order spoil their fun? A little, perhaps. But sacrificing temporary enjoyment for the sake of something much more important was worth it. We see life through finite eyes, but God sees the greater good.

Inward Glimpse

Heavenly Father, thank You for Christ's example of setting one's desires aside for the greater good. Help me follow His example with a joyful attitude. Amen.

- How do you typically respond when circumstances require you to change your plans? What must happen so that Christ is reflected in your response?

- Write a prayer asking God to help you embrace and obey His will for your life day by day.

Outward Glance

Father, I pray that _____ will embrace Your will for her life. May she follow Christ's example and surrender everything to You. May she embrace the conviction that her food is to do Your will and to finish whatever You want to do through her (John 4:34). Amen.

One More Peek

Father, if you are willing, take this cup from me; yet not my will, but yours be done (Luke 22:42).

Weep with Those
Who Weep

*"With everlasting kindness
I will have compassion on you,"
says the* LORD *your Redeemer.*

ISAIAH 54:8

Upward Gaze

God, I praise You for being gracious and compassionate.
You are slow to anger and rich in love. You're good to all.
You have compassion on all You have made (Psalm 145:8-
9). Thank You for understanding my pain. Amen.

∼

Billy Graham once said, "We must never minimize the suffering of
another. Scripture's mandate to us is, 'Weep with them that weep'"
(Romans 12:15 KJV).

That's a tall order. Weeping with those who weep might require
rearranging our schedules. It might mean being quick to listen and

slow to speak. It might even require setting aside personal prejudices or pain.

My friend Joy has done all those things. She and her husband married young and wanted to have children. After several years of trying unsuccessfully to conceive, they visited an infertility clinic. Doctors asked questions, poked, and prodded. "We find no definitive reason for your inability to become pregnant," they said.

Joy found the diagnosis difficult to accept. Each month when her hopes were dashed, she curled up and allowed herself the freedom to cry. She watched her friends raise their children and wished that she too could experience motherhood.

One afternoon Joy visited a woman whom she'd been getting to know. The conversation turned to intimate issues, and Joy's new friend confided that she'd had more than five abortions.

How could you? thought Joy. *I can only dream of becoming pregnant, and you do this?* Before she uttered a word, however, she caught the pain and fear of condemnation in the woman's eyes. A passionate love and concern overwhelmed Joy and squelched critical thoughts. "Are you okay?" she whispered.

The woman broke down. She rocked back and forth as silent sobs wracked her body. Tears flooded her face.

Joy waited silently until the woman calmed and then she gently rubbed her back. "I love you," she said. Sensing the woman's desire for solitude, she left. Since that day, their friendship has grown, and more post-abortive women have entered Joy's life (learn more about Joy at www.joydekok.com).

It would be easy for Joy, an infertile woman, to harbor jealousy or bitterness or to minimize the suffering of those who conceive and abort. Instead, she reassures them of God's forgiveness and hope. She listens to their stories, encourages them, cries with them, and walks with them along their healing journey. And they, in turn, find the courage to share their experience with others bearing similar pain or considering abortion.

Joy's willingness to weep with those who weep models Christ's example. He too entered others' pain. When He visited Mary and Martha after their brother's death, Mary fell at His feet. "Lord, if You had been here, my brother would not have died," she said, sobbing. Her Jewish friends stood nearby, tears coursing down their cheeks.

Jesus felt Mary's heartache and understood the Jews' pain. He didn't minimize their emotions. Rather, two words describe His response: Jesus wept (John 11:32-36).

Sometimes our schedules and personal concerns consume us, or we simply grow immune to other people's pain. We hear the grim late-night news, and then we turn off the television and go to bed without giving it a second thought. We drive down the street and see the homeless squatting on the sidewalk. We hear about neighbors or church friends who are ill or hospitalized. How do we respond?

"I would rather feel compassion than know the meaning of it," said Thomas Aquinas. The world would be a different place if everyone held the same perspective. Granted, we can't rush to everyone's rescue, but we can do what we're able.

We can pray with a mother who's devastated at her teenager's spiritual condition. We can send a care package to a homesick college student or soldier overseas. We can invite a military spouse or single parent and his or her children to join our family for dinner or a fun activity. We can provide transportation to medical appointments for a woman suffering with chronic illness. We can ask the Lord to give us His heart for people.

When we weep with those who weep, we fulfill God's mandate. We show that we feel compassion rather than simply know the meaning of it. And we make a difference in someone's life for eternity.

Inward Glimpse

Dear Father, thank You for being a God who cares deeply about people. Please give me Your heart for those around me. Amen.

- Name someone you know who is experiencing difficulty. List two things you can do to show that you care.
- Name three ways God has displayed His compassion for you through other people.

Outward Glance

Father, I pray that _____ will clothe herself with compassion, kindness, humility, gentleness, and patience (Colossians 3:12). Teach her to forgive others just as Christ has forgiven her (Ephesians 4:32). Amen.

One More Peek

For I was hungry and you gave me something to eat, I was thirsty and you gave me something to drink, I was a stranger and you invited me in, I needed clothes and you clothed me, I was sick and you looked after me, I was in prison and you came to visit me (Matthew 25:35-36).

The Language
of Kindness

*Make sure that nobody pays back wrong for wrong,
but always try to be kind to each other and to everyone else.*

1 THESSALONIANS 5:15

Upward Gaze

God, I praise You for displaying Your kindness and love for
me in the person of Jesus Christ. You saved me, not because
of righteous things I've done but because of Your mercy
(Titus 3:4-5). I'm eternally grateful. Amen.

~

Someone once said, "Kindness is a language that the deaf can hear
and the blind can see." That's a great definition! It infers that kindness—
love in action—is a powerful force, and rightly so. A listening ear, an
encouraging word, a helping hand, an appropriate gift—even the
smallest kind act communicates a message that spans age differences,
gender, and nationality and brings hope and healing to hurting people.

Opportunities to speak this language surround us. Jeanette used it recently after meeting a woman at a church-sponsored barbecue. During their conversation, the woman told Jeanette about herself— divorced, raising her eight-year-old daughter, recently laid off from work. Then she spilled the cruncher—she'd just discovered she was pregnant.

Jeanette cringed at her own initial response. *You've ruined your life,* she thought. But a still, small voice rebuked her.

Jesus' attitude isn't like that.

The words instantly changed Jeanette's perspective. *That's right. She made a poor choice, but it hasn't destroyed her. Jesus still loves her, even though He doesn't condone what she's done.*

Jeanette wanted to reflect Jesus' attitude. *How can I do that?* she wondered. The answer came quickly: Show kindness. She recalled the woman saying her finances were so tight that she couldn't afford any extras for her little girl. Then Jeanette remembered the cash gift her parents had given her recently. *I'll give her a portion so she can feel free to buy her daughter something special now and again, like an ice cream treat on a hot summer day!*

Jeanette pursued her idea. To the single, pregnant mom who recognized her wrong and felt condemned for her choice, that simple act of kindness communicated a concrete reminder of God's love.

Scripture teems with stories of people speaking the language of kindness. In the Old Testament, we read about a Moabite woman named Ruth. Poor gal—she'd recently buried her husband, her brother-in-law, and her father-in-law. Then she moved from Moab to Judah with her mother-in-law. She abandoned everything familiar— her family, her culture, her language—and entered a foreign land empty-handed. To feed herself and her mother-in-law, she followed barley reapers and gleaned what they missed.

Things weren't looking too promising for Ruth until the day Boaz, the field's owner, saw her. He'd heard about the respect this foreigner had shown to her mother-in-law, and he rewarded her for it. He provided drinking water, told the reapers to leave extra sheaves, and instructed the servants not to touch her.

Ruth understood the language of kindness Boaz spoke. "May I continue to find favor in your eyes, my lord," she said. "You have given me comfort and have spoken kindly to your servant—though I do not have the standing of one of your servant girls" (Ruth 2:13). She appreciated his favor and acknowledged that it comforted her in this difficult season of her life.

It's easy to speak the language of kindness to those who understand and respond. But sometimes the recipient regards us with suspicion. Perhaps she's been deceived in the past by someone who showed kindness but had selfish motives, and she needs time to heal. When that happens, we can ask God for wisdom, for patience, and for Him to embrace that person with His love in other ways too.

Regardless of how busy we are, we can include kindness in our everyday vocabulary. Like Jeanette, we can share finances or material possessions with those less fortunate. We can donate blankets or coats to the homeless or sponsor a child overseas through programs like Compassion International. We can offer to take a neighbor's children to Sunday school, encourage a child who struggles with academics, or visit a shut in.

The language of kindness communicates God's love. Let's ask Him to open our eyes and ears so we might recognize those who need to hear it most.

Inward Glimpse

Dear Father, thank You for Your kindness to me. Help me, in turn, speak the language of kindness to others. Amen.

- List five kindnesses that God has shown you.
- List five kind acts you can do for others. Purpose to do them!

Outward Glance

Father, I pray that _____ will add brotherly kindness and love to her godliness. Make her effective and productive in her knowledge of the Lord Jesus Christ (2 Peter 1:7-8). Amen.

One More Peek

And now I will show you the most excellent way. If I speak in the tongues of men and of angels, but have not love, I am only a resounding gong or a clanging cymbal (1 Corinthians 12:31–13:1).

Silence

Be still, and know that I am God;
I will be exalted among the nations,
I will be exalted in the earth.

PSALM 46:10

Upward Gaze

Father, in the busyness of each day, my soul finds rest in You alone. My hope and my salvation come from You. I praise You, for You alone are my fortress and my stronghold (Psalm 62:5-6). Amen.

∾

Stars speckled the sky and sparkled like diamonds. Moonlight flooded the harbor and danced across its salty ripples. Only the gentle slap-slap of the waves against the rocky shoreline broke the silence. Creation's beauty filled my senses as I surveyed it from my bedroom window. But something far more precious filled my spirit—God's glorious, all-absorbing presence.

Fifteen minutes earlier, something, or perhaps more accurately, Someone, woke me. His presence was so real, so near, that I instantly asked, *What is it, God? What do You want? Does someone specific need prayer?* No name came to mind. Instead, I felt drawn to the window.

As I gazed at the surreal scene before me, a quiet thought entered my mind. *I woke you because I want to tell you something, Grace. Be still. Listen.* I scarcely dared to breathe lest I shatter the moment's reverence.

Do you see those stars? I know everything about them. I created them. I named them. But Grace, you're far more precious to Me than those stars. You are mine, and I will accomplish all that concerns you.

I stood transfixed in the presence of the living God, invigorated at the clarity with which He spoke, reassured of His love, and excited by His promise. I spent the next hour praising Him, reading His Word, and recording the incident in my journal lest a single detail be forgotten.

The experience left me hungry for deeper communion with God, for the ability to hear His voice again and again and again. And it reminded me that it's much easier to hear Him in the silence than in the hubbub of my busy world.

Silence—an unknown entity in the rush and rumble of everyday life. From dawn till dusk, exterior noise surrounds us—round-the-clock freeway traffic, the neighbor's dog, our teenager's CD player, a coworker's radio, crying babies, televisions, phones, doorbells, sirens, airplanes.

But we also battle inner noise. We worry about our kids, we rehash old arguments, we juggle our agendas. *Reschedule the dentist appointment. Buy a birthday gift. Remember Junior's baseball practice. Hem hubby's new pants. Hire a babysitter. Phone Grandma.* The racket rushes in and around us. It invades the stillness and snatches our opportunities to hear God's voice.

In her book *Open Heart, Open Home*, Karen Burton Mains writes this:

> In order to hear His voice we must remove ourselves regularly
> from the busy, overly active, exciting, troublesome outside
> world. Contemplation, the fastening of one's mind on one's

Creator, is the only method by which we can properly develop this interior silence and openness to the spirit.[16]

How can we do this? By setting aside regular times alone, perhaps 15 minutes once or twice a week, to bask in God's presence. We may have to do this while the baby is napping or when the kids are playing outside. We may have to do it before going to bed at night, when everyone else is sleeping. In any case, we come to Him with no agenda—not even prayer. We shut out all other concerns and focus on Him alone. Our only purpose is to praise Him, to listen for His voice, and to obey.

In the silence, God may give directives for ministry or relationships. He might bring an encouraging Scripture verse to mind. He may convict of a need for inner correction. Or He might be quiet. "I began to learn that the silence was in itself the voice of God," Karen writes. "This is the quiet of the Spirit, a communication which occurs without words."

Our minds aren't accustomed to silence. It feels awkward. We rush to fill the void with busy thoughts, but we must learn to be still. And that takes time. Yes, my dear, in the middle of our busy lives, we must make time for silence. For in it, we can hear God's voice. And when we listen and obey, He fills us with a greater understanding of who He is, and He makes our lives beacons of light to those around us.

Inward Glimpse

Father, thank You for wanting to speak to me. Help me make time for silent contemplation. Open my ears to hear and my heart to obey. Amen.

- Ask the Lord to help you make time for quiet contemplation. Plan a strategy! Start with 15 minutes per week so you don't feel overwhelmed. Don't be discouraged if busy thoughts crowd your mind at first. Just bring them back to the Lord. Like any other worthwhile endeavor, this takes practice.

- Read the hymn "The Quiet Hour." List at least four things that the writer hoped would happen as he sought fellowship with the Lord in the stillness.

Outward Glance

Dear Father, I pray that _____ will practice the discipline of listening for Your voice. Just as Samuel heard You speak in the night, may she hear Your voice and say as Samuel did, "Speak, for your servant is listening" (1 Samuel 3:10). Amen.

One More Peek

Do not be quick with your mouth,
do not be hasty in your heart
to utter anything before God.
God is in heaven
and you are on earth,
so let your words be few (Ecclesiastes 5:2).

The Quiet Hour

E. May Grimes

Speak, Lord, in the stillness,
While I wait on Thee;
Hushed my heart to listen,
In expectancy.

Speak, O blessed Master,
In this quiet hour;
Let me see Thy face, Lord,
Feel Thy touch of power.

For the words Thou speakest,
They are life indeed;
Living bread from heaven,
Now my spirit feed.

All to Thee is yielded,
I am not my own;
Blissful, glad surrender,
I am Thine alone.

Speak, Thy servant heareth,
Be not silent, Lord;
Waits my soul upon Thee
For the quickening word.

Fill me with the knowledge
Of Thy glorious will;
All Thine own good pleasure
In Thy child fulfill.

Heavenly Search and Rescue

For the Son of Man came to seek
and to save what was lost.

LUKE 19:10

Upward Gaze

God, my heart rejoices in knowing that You came to seek and save what was lost. Your love is so great, so rich, and so free toward me—You gave everything so that we might be in relationship. Because You sought me, I will seek You. I will look to Your strength and seek Your face always (1 Chronicles 16:11). Amen.

~

On a recent hotel stay, I enjoyed reading a book for a couple of hours in the lobby. While there, I overheard the desk clerk converse with guests. Her enthusiasm sparkled: "Yes, sir, what can I do for you? You need extra towels? I'll have someone deliver them right away. Have a wonderful afternoon!"

Encourage her, an inner voice prompted. So I did. I approached her desk and said, "Has anyone ever told you that you're masterful at what you do?"

The young woman looked pleased. "Thank you," she said. "I love my job." She glanced at my book. "What are you reading?"

"*Knowing God by Name,*" I said.

Her eyes popped and her mouth started moving. Fast. "I went to church with my new boyfriend yesterday. If the preacher's words are true, I'm not saved. But I'm beginning to understand what he said. You know—about Jesus dying on the cross for my sins.

"I stopped drinking alcohol ten years ago. I stopped smoking too. I couldn't do that on my own—only God could do it for me. And if He could do that, I know He can do anything, so I'm wide open to finding out more about Him."

Now *my* eyes popped. God was obviously working in this woman's heart, and He'd arranged circumstances so she could learn more about Him that afternoon. Isn't that exciting?

God loves people more than words can say. Jesus' life, death, and resurrection prove His desire for a relationship with us. Today's key verse tells us that He seeks us. And because He's God, He knows a zillion ways to do that...

A weary corporate executive opens a drawer in her hotel room. She pulls out a Gideon Bible and begins to read the book of John. She's heard Christ's name but mostly as an expletive. Now she discovers Him as a person, a friend, a Savior.

A drug-addicted teen searches for something—anything that lends meaning to her abused existence. She stuffs a backpack, leaves home without a backward glance, and hitchhikes to the big city. Guess who offers her a ride? A pastor's wife with a passion for kids and Jesus.

Two couples sit in a hospital waiting room while their youngsters undergo major surgery. They swap stories and share tears. One couple prays aloud for the children. The other sees serenity and senses peace. Later, they exchange phone calls and e-mails. A friendship builds, and several months later, those parents receive Christ into their lives.

Sometimes God, in His mercy, reaches men and women through a stranger's words, a neighbor's thoughtful deed, a magazine article, or a song. If you're reading this and don't yet know Him, guess what? Perhaps He put this book in your hands because He's seeking *you*!

If you've already found Him, He wants your relationship to grow more intimate. He also wants your availability. As He seeks those who don't know Him, perhaps He wants to use your hands to show kindness, your mouth to speak life-giving truth, or your feet to carry the gospel to distant lands where His word has never been heard.

We can find *huge* encouragement in knowing that the God of the universe seeks a relationship with us. He created us for that purpose. When sin entered the world and destroyed that possibility, He sent Jesus Christ to bridge the gap. Christ's death paid the price for our sin so we could once again enjoy fellowship with God. And His resurrection purchased a place in heaven for us so we can spend eternity with the Father.

It's difficult for our human minds to understand that God values and seeks us. But Scripture says it's true. A heavenly search and rescue happens every day, and we're the ones He's looking for.

Inward Glimpse

Dear Father, thank You for seeking a relationship with me. Help me understand the value You place on it. Amen.

- List three ways in which God has sought a relationship with you.
- Describe your relationship with God today. Where would you like it to be? What changes must take place in order for that to happen?

Outward Glance

Father, please help _____ understand that You desire a relationship with her. Give her a desire to respond. May she serve You with a wholehearted devotion and a willing mind (1 Chronicles 28:9). Teach her to look to Your face and Your strength forever (1 Chronicles 16:11). Amen.

One More Peek

Come near to God and he will come near to you (James 4:8).

A Closing Thought

My dear sister,

No matter your background or present situation, God loves you and wants to enjoy an eternal relationship with *you*, beginning today. How is that possible? Simply by confessing your sin and acknowledging your need for a Savior.

Jesus Christ, God's perfect Son, is that Savior. He paid your death penalty for sin when He died on the cross, and He purchased a place in heaven for you when He rose from the grave three days later. Trusting Him for eternal life is the most important decision you'll ever make and one you'll never regret.

I sealed my decision with a simple prayer that went like this:

> *"Lord Jesus Christ, I know I'm a sinner and don't deserve eternal life. But I believe You died and rose from the grave to purchase a place in heaven for me. Jesus, come into my life. Take control of my life. Forgive my sins and save me. I turn from anything that is not pleasing to You and place my trust in You for salvation. I accept the free gift of eternal life. Amen."*

Praying this prayer won't make your life problem-free, but it guarantees an eternal relationship with the One who created you for a purpose and loves you more than words can say. It launches a faith journey unlike anything you've ever experienced. If you've entered that relationship, I've love to offer encouragement. Please feel free to contact me through my website: www.gracefox.com.

Know you are loved,

Grace

Endnotes

1. Phillip Keller, *A Shepherd Looks at Psalm 23* (Grand Rapids, MI: Zondervan Publishing House, 1979), pp. 44-45.

2. Ramona Cramer Tucker, "Loose Lips," *Today's Christian Woman*, Nov./Dec. 2000, p. 102.

3. Kilian J. Healy, *Walking with God* (New York: Declan X. McMullen Co., 1948), p. 35.

4. Tricia McCrary Rhodes, *The Soul at Rest* (Minneapolis: Bethany House Publishers, 1996), p. 86.

5. David Augsburger, *The Freedom of Forgiveness* (Chicago: Moody Press, 1970), p. 40.

6. Personal interview.

7. Donna Partow, *Walking in Total God-Confidence* (Minneapolis: Bethany House Publishers, 1999), p. 134.

8. Michele Orecklin, "At What Cost Beauty?" *Time*, Canadian edition, March 1, 2004, p. 42.

9. Karen Burton Mains, *Open Heart, Open Home* (Elgin, IL: David C. Cook Publishing Co., 1976), pp. 25-26.

10. Andrew Murray, *Waiting on God* (Chicago: Moody Press), p. 119.

11. Ibid.

12. Kay Arthur, *The Sovereignty of God* (Chattanooga, TN: Precept Ministries International, 1997), p. 23.

13. John Ortberg, *If You Want to Walk on Water You've Got to Get Out of the Boat* (Grand Rapids, MI: Zondervan Publishing House, 2001), pp. 150-151.

14. Nancy Leigh DeMoss, *Surrender: The Heart God Controls* (Chicago: Moody Publishers, 2003), p. 112.

15. Rick Warren, *The Purpose-Driven Life* (Grand Rapids, MI: Zondervan, 2002), p. 139.

16. Mains, *Open Heart, Open Home*, p. 192.